Everything you Need to Know to Survive Teaching

Related titles

100 Essential Lists for Teachers – Duncan Grey

Teacher's Survival Guide: Second Edition – Angela Thody, Derek Bowden and Barbara Gray

Sue Cowley's Teaching Clinic – Sue Cowley

Guerilla Guide to Teaching – Sue Cowley

Everything you Need to Know to Survive Teaching

Ranting Teacher

continuum
LONDON • NEW YORK

Continuum International Publishing Group
The Tower Building   15 East 26th Street
11 York Road   New York
London SE1 7NX   NY 10010

British Library Cataloguing-in-Publication Data
A catalogue record for this book is available from the British Library.

ISBN: 08264 7534 5 (paperback)

Library of Congress Cataloguing-in-Publicaton Data
A catalog record for this book is available from the Library of Congress.

Typeset by Acorn Bookwork Ltd, Salisbury, Wiltshire
Printed and bound in Great Britain by Hobbs the Printers, Hampshire

Contents

Introduction: Why do you want to be a teacher?

This is a question that you, the potential teacher, or trainee teacher, or practising teacher, will have been asked. Your response will vary, depending on whether you are trying to impress somebody, are being honest, or you've just had a bad day.

At first, it may just be your friends, incredulous and drop-jawed, who choke on their pints as you celebrate the end of your finals, after you have dropped the bombshell of your plans for life post-graduation. You may have just left school yourself, and while your friends are off plugging the gaps in their year, you have decided to enrol for an education degree. It could be your parents asking this question, after you've informed them that you're giving up your go-getting job in marketing for something less soulless. Or your partner, detecting a midlife crisis after twenty years of boring yet lucrative banking or brokering, or travelling or child-raising, or whatever it is you've been doing with your life.

Maybe you are that partner or friend or parent of a teacher, who sees the teacher in their life come home exhausted, shell-shocked, angry, or sometimes elated, and has uttered that question on a regular basis as the teacher you know settles down to mark a pile of coursework or run through some statistics when they could be spending quality time with their own children, or down the pub with their mates, or doing something more sporting or cultural than correcting spelling mistakes.

Teachers are asked this question throughout their careers. You, the teacher, must know your true answer. Maybe you can't really articulate why you want to be a teacher, but you should have an answer ready to trot out for every situation. You will be asked by interviewers, who will be looking for certain qualities. You'll be asked by the children that you teach, especially when you look harassed and fed up. And you'll ask yourself, frequently, especially after a bad day.

The truth is, there must be a million ways to answer this question. Interviewers must have heard myriad responses and variations. Is there a correct answer? Probably not. Maybe they're just curious, feeling a little jaded themselves, having lived through times when behaviour is getting worse, demands are getting tougher, respect is plummeting, and the salary won't cover the mortgage on a garden shed.

You may pick up this book expecting it to be full of rants. You'll be right. Think of it as a worst-case scenario handbook for teaching. However, this is not the extreme edge of teaching; rather, this is the kind of thing that teachers put up with every term, or week, or day. You may be the Mary Poppins of teachers, who never has any problems and whose intentions are only ever of the noblest kind, but look around your staffroom: someone in there may well be asking themselves on a daily basis if it's all worth it. Maybe you should slip them a copy of this book to cheer them up, to make them realize they're not alone, or to remind them of some of the tricks of the trade that are buried deep down and can be tapped into to get a handle on a situation.

In *Four Essays on Liberty: Political Ideas in the Twentieth Century* (Oxford University Press, 1969), Sir Isaiah Berlin wrote, 'Injustice, poverty, slavery, ignorance – these may be cured by reform or revolution. But men do not live only by fighting evils. They live by positive goals, individual and collective, a vast variety of them, seldom predictable, at times incompatible'. I can't promise you reform or revolution. But I can help in fighting evils, and you don't even need a superhero costume. The positive goals in this book take the form of 'Top tips', to be found in each section, so that for every negative there is some kind of positive, or, as the twee phrase goes, you can turn your frown upside down.

Top tips

So we come back to the original question. Why *do you* want to be a teacher? Why do you want to start training? Why do you want to carry on in your job? Why do you want that promotion, when you know it means more hours, more hassles, and not much more pay? Define your own answer. If you don't know what your answer is, it's easy to lose your way. Know your answer, recite it like a positive affirmation, even if all you can think of right now is, 'Well, the holiday's are good'.

Enjoy this book. You may empathize, sympathize, or know far better, but hopefully it will give you some ideas that you can use or adapt in the classroom. Or if you aren't a teacher, it may make you appreciate your own slice of life a little bit more.

1 On your marks: The trials of training

The peculiar process of interviewing

Interviews for teaching jobs are in a league of their own when it comes to tiring and unnecessary trials. Attend an interview for a teaching job and you would never believe that teachers are in short supply or that there is a hint of the so-called recruitment crisis we are always hearing about.

Teaching interviews are designed to be demoralizing, tiring, and very often tests in toadying – in short, all the things you will come to expect from the job once you secure it.

First of all there's the application form. Or CV and covering letter. Or both if you're unlucky. Each form can take a couple of hours to fill in, with personal details and statements about why you want to teach, your experience, your philosophy on education, and many more hoops to jump through before you can be considered for a shortlist.

Schools often have a quick turn-around between the closing date and the interviews, sometimes only a couple of days. This can come as a shock when you first start applying for jobs, and if you apply for several with the same closing dates then you may find yourself asked for more than one interview on the same day. Worse than this is the school's expectation that if you are offered the job, you will have to accept or decline there and then. Many schools do this, which means that if you have interviews lined up for Tuesday, Wednesday and Thursday you have to take a gamble. If the first school offers you the job, but you liked the sound of the third school best, do you stick with the first offer or throw it away and hope you get offered the job you really want? Of course, you could risk offending or denial by asking for a couple of days to think about it, or even risk being struck from a local authority's good books by accepting a job and then withdrawing your offer.

At the end of a day's interviewing, candidates are not often of sound mind to make such weighty decisions anyway. This is because of the trials they must endure during the day. Many interview days will be variations of the following scenario.

Firstly, there's the arrival. Suited and booted, you arrive at the school and are dumped in reception or the staffroom along with the other candidates, with whom you will be expected to make polite conversation for the rest of the day, while hiding your interview strategies and trying to glean any information they have. This is by far the worst part of the whole process. Some candidates are masters in undermining your confidence and appear certain to get the job from the start. They may sicken you with their constant sucking up to existing staff by asking intelligent or obvious questions. They may tell you horror stories about situations they have deftly handled, rumours they have heard about the school, and boast of a wide range of experience all gained in the first few months of teaching practice.

You will normally have a timetable of things to do during the day, which could include making a positive impression on your possible future colleagues, and looking cool to the kids who may have a say in whether they want you teaching them. You could well have to teach a short lesson to a random class in front of senior teachers, who will keep your immaculate handouts for their own use and expect you to believe that all the children are as well behaved as this specially selected lot.

Then there are the actual interviews, which could be called informal chats or formal interviews, and could be with just two people or up to a dozen. These range from heads of department to headteachers and governors, and this is where you are expected to trot out your carefully prepared answers on anything and everything to do with teaching and yourself. Once you attend your fifth school interview you should have a pretty good idea of every possible question that could arise, but also the horrible feeling when you answer that this is purgatory and you have to repeat your actions again and again until you get it right. You will also notice that your answers sound more and more like a script.

After a day of school tours, informal and formal interviews, short lesson teaching where you demonstrate every style and groovy trick you've picked up so far, smiling behind gritted teeth at the other candidates to show you're a team player, asking interesting questions, looking keen and eager as the kids barge round the canteen at lunchtime, enjoying the weak coffee and even weaker salad that is your day's subsistence, there comes crunch time. The interview panel take another hour deliberating over which candidate looked like they could handle the children, sucked up the most, and could last the longest without rushing to the toilet (one of the most

essential skills in teaching), during which time you have
to engage in more small talk with your sweaty-palmed
co-interviewees. If you have lasted this long, you will be
so sick of hearing about the school and staring at the
same bit of staffroom wall and smiling at the existing
teachers in case they have a say in your appointment, and
will be so eager to leave, that if you are turned down for
the post it will feel like a relief anyway.

Top tips

Be aware that you're playing a game like some ancient
courtly ritual. There are procedures that the school will
follow during the recruitment process that only get
dusted off for that particular tradition, and equally you
will be expected to carry out procedures that seem
obvious or obscure. Go with the flow. It's all good practice at working under pressure.

Learn to read between the lines and decide if the school
sounds like the kind of place you want to teach in
anyway. If the school secretary has sent you out the
wrong information, or just an application form with no
departmental information, then consider how this most
important first impression has failed. And then remember
that this will be the same secretary who will be responsible for passing on important messages to you, submitting
your bank details to the local authority, and so on. Fair
enough that you are trying to make a good first impression on your potential employers and colleagues, but if
the school, with all their experience in recruitment, can't
get it right, then why waste your time.

Adapt your details according to the school. Don't
include statements emphasizing your firm belief in mixed

ability teaching if the school sets pupils from the moment they enter. You may have to do your research here. If you're not sent enough information about the place, then look up their website or last inspection report.

As for surviving the day itself, you will learn to formulate your own strategies once you've attended a few interviews. Or you may get lucky and only ever attend one interview, in which case any further advice isn't required! Just be prepared for an exhausting day, and practise smiling sincerely.

Incentives to train

Gone are the days of merely trying to persuade people to teach with an advertising campaign. Now there's real hard cash being thrown around to attract graduates to sign up for a PGCE (Post Graduate Certificate in Education).

Which advert would persuade you to teach? I can't remember if there was a moment when I sat in the cinema, saw a finely crafted piece of propaganda and, without raising my eyes to the roof, thought, 'Yes, that's it! Who would have thought that getting in early to see "Jurassic Park 8" would have opened my eyes to a career I had never before contemplated!'.

One of the Teacher Training Agency's recent advertisements featured lots of headless people and the soundtrack of the seven dwarves singing 'Hi-ho hi-ho, it's off to work we go'. The headless people were muffled, presumably because you need a head to speak, and so the sounds of ringing phones and factory machinery dominated. Okay, so 'headless woman' may have been addressing a group of boring old executives, but there are at least lots of positive things in this scenario. For example, headless woman gets to wear a skirt to work if she chooses, because she doesn't have to climb on tables to fix the window blinds that never shut properly. Headless woman also has a flipchart! – with colour pens! No scratchy old blackboard for her! But the biggest bonus is that Miss Fancy-Skirt-and-Flipchart also has a captive audience. I bet there's no shouting out or heckling from those old boys. Unless they are MPs, of course, but they seem pretty well behaved in the advert.

After a montage of nightmare scenarios that could be your job if you don't immediately sign up to be a teacher, like taking the heads off dolls on a factory disassembly line (and I'm sure I had a job just like that to try and make ends meet while at college), we are suddenly shown normality. Well, screen normality anyway. The jolly laughter of merry children enjoying their science lesson as a young, yet balding, man rubs his pate and laughs along because the experiment (something to do with electrical charges giving you a bad hair day) wouldn't work for him.

Now, I don't know about you, but I'm not sure what type of message this is giving out. After all, us over-educated types have been taught to analyse everything, and it's a habit that sometimes inhibits the enjoyment of books and films. But I do think there's something inherently wrong with this current advert – is it saying that the only way Mr Prematurely Bald gets female attention is by teaching giggling schoolgirls? Or that it's OK to take the piss out of your teacher and their appearance because they are so easygoing? There are many readings of any text, including the script of this advert. But it's easy to pull carefully crafted adverts to pieces. So let's do it again.

It's time to move on from the Mr Chipsesque 'Everyone remembers a good teacher' type of advertisement. I still reckon that bad teachers are the ones that stick in my mind. I remember doing my own version of the 'Those that can, teach' recruitment adverts. It went something like: 'Can you give up every evening to mark piles of half-arsed pieces of homework? Can you take abuse from children and their parents on a daily basis? Can you relearn on a continual basis, every time the government throws some new initiative at you? Can you manage to work with poor resources?' And so on. It's quite simple to do, and I'm sure any teacher will have their own 'Can you?' lists.

Anyway, I'd like to suggest my own ideas for the next teacher recruitment adverts. I mean, why should those poor overpaid headless corporate types at the advertising agencies stress themselves about these matters when they should be out there polishing their BMWs? So, in the spirit of appealing to the generation who have grown up with extreme sports like snowboarding, and everything else extreme, from computer console games to cheesy strings, I present: 'Extreme teaching'.

The scene opens on a blanket of snow, and our view of the scene is somewhat obscured by flurries of snow. Then we begin to focus, and see our hero teacher bundled up in trendy jacket and stripy hat and gloves. Teacher is directing the poor shivering children onto their buses as they smile gratefully at her. Cue a graphic of a stamp leaving its impression on the scene, reading 'Extreme bus duties'.

Scene two would show manic children running down corridors, leaving slopping wet puddles behind them as they go, until they run into the smiling face of their teacher, who has a jolly laugh with them while directing them into a classroom where children are calmly playing and there isn't a paper aeroplane or crisp wrapper in sight. The graphic of the stamp again leaves an impression on the scene, which this time reads, 'Extreme wet break'.

A couple more similar scenes would then lead up to the clincher, which would probably be a scene of our intrepid teachers on a ski slope in Andorra with their laughing charges, and not an underage cigarette in view, as the voiceover says something like, 'Extreme teaching – are you up for it?'

Yes, it's still a sanitized version of the job. But who would carry on teaching if it was all so dire? And why else would graduates flock to sign up for training courses? Oh, yes, the money.

Top tips

From headless factory worker to golden handshakes, golden handcuffs and other glittering body parts, the Teacher Training Agency has turned to alchemy to recruit teachers. If you're about to sign up for a PGCE, there are two things you need to be crystal clear about.

Firstly, make sure you know exactly what you are entitled to. Rules and incentives are changing all the time, as the demand for particular subjects changes and the number of children in the population rises or falls. Don't be seduced by the advertising and fail to read the small print. It may seem like a good idea to do a PGCE to pay off some of your degree course debts, but some-times the money being offered will only go into your bank account once you have passed the course, or worked for a certain number of years. Be aware of the conditions that apply, and that you will, after all, have to complete a particularly demanding course and then do a job that requires more than waiting for each pay day to come round.

Secondly, once you're in a school, don't gloat about all the money falling your way because your subject is now designated a shortage subject. Someone in that staffroom, someone with just a few more years' experience than you, someone who did the job for the love not the money (but wouldn't mind the money either) will probably be taking home less money than you every month. They won't have benefited from having their student loans paid off, or a 'golden hello', and they don't need continual reminders that they have a huge reason to resent you!

The mentor – make or break time

When you train to be a teacher, and are thrown to the lions that are 7B just before lunchtime on a wet Wednesday, you are given somebody to hold your hand and guide you along the rocky path that leads to Qualified Teacher Status (QTS). This is your mentor, an existing teacher of the subject or age group, and this person will have an enormous effect on your personal development, approaches to teaching and paperwork, and to be frank, whether you stick it out at all.

To understand why the mentor can be so influential, we have to look into the mindset and motivation of the mentor. Why do they take on board these duties? There could be several reasons, or a combination of them all.

The mentor could be the philanthropic sort. An experienced and successful teacher, this mentor does her job well and knows it. She looks at some of her colleagues who struggle to interest the pupils, and knows that if she passes on her wisdom to the next generation of teachers, everyone will benefit. There is nothing boastful about her, however; she is calm in a crisis, constructive in her criticism, as well as being encouraging, organized and resourceful. If you are about to embark on a school placement, then pray that you are assigned a mentor like this, and that she or he is not tainted by any of the other more negative traits that a mentor could possess. This mentor will bring out the best in you, and you will carry their worldly wisdom with you throughout your career.

The egotistical mentor may share many traits with the ideal mentor, but their motivation for taking on this responsibility does not spring from the same still waters. This mentor may well be a very good teacher, and as such, her demands will be high. She doesn't suffer fools gladly, neither will she see that there are many ways to deliver the same learning objective, because she knows that her way is best. If she silences a class because her reputation precedes her, she will not understand why you struggle. She may well be glad to see that her trainee charges cannot command silence with one raise of an eyebrow, because this only reinforces her feelings of self-importance and belief that she is perfect and universally respected. Any advice may be given to the student teachers in a very patronizing way, but saccharine-coated, because deep down she is conflicted. She wants her trainees to do well, of course, because this reflects well on her mentoring abilities, but at the same time she could not bear to see any of them put into practice their fancy college ways, enlightened by teaching theories that she hasn't had time to swot up on. Probably because she spent too much time practising raising an eyebrow in front of the mirror.

One step beyond the egotistical mentor is the patronizing mentor. This teacher probably didn't want the role of looking after student teachers, maybe because he feels he has far too much on his plate without anything else, even if it does give him an extra free period each week. He could well seize the opportunity to offload his most difficult classes onto his trainees, telling them that if they survive this, then everything else will be a doddle. He will overuse the phrases 'Told you so' and 'See what I mean'. His advice and criticism may well hinder your progress, and he will dismiss any of the new teaching methods you learned about at college as just a fad, preferring as he does the 'chalk and talk' approach. The worst thing you could do with this type of mentor is argue back. The best thing to do is to ignore his arcane advice, take on board anything of use that he may come up with (there's bound to be something in there somewhere), listen to why the kids complain about him and ensure you don't do the same thing.

Another unfortunate situation with a mentor is the personality clash. This happens in any walk of life, but in a mentor-trainee relationship, it can be damaging. Training to be a teacher is a stressful course, and mentors may not always understand every shock to the system that their trainee is experiencing. They may have their own agenda. Maybe mentoring is just a stepping stone for them, a way to achieve a promotion or to gain release from some of their teaching duties. Similarly, you as the trainee may not understand their disbelief when you fail to set a homework task yet again, or didn't get the worksheets for your lesson photocopied on time, or didn't prepare for your lesson properly because you felt the need to have a beer with your fellow trainees to discuss how awful your mentors are. Personality clashes happen, and if you find yourself in this situation, then don't do anything to antagonize it.

The school-based mentor has a huge influence over the trainee's success, even down to whether they pass or fail the teacher training course. The college tutor will visit the trainee in the school, watch them teach, inspect their paperwork, interview them about the way they are developing, and so on, but the tutor will also liaise with the mentor, and only tick the right boxes with the mentor's approval. The mentor keeps records, writes out lesson observations, and continually assesses the trainee's every move, from planning schemes of work to interacting with the pupils.

Not only this, but the working relationship between mentor and trainee can sometimes influence the trainee's decision as to whether to complete the course or not. Many trainee teachers drop out of the course not because they find the course too difficult, or the kids too demanding, but because their mentor is a bitch.

Top tips

Be aware that the school mentor may have their own agenda for taking on mentoring duties. The sooner you realize that their constant criticisms of the way you do things could well be down to their own insecurities, then the happier you will become. Or maybe you do need to look at how you're doing. You will have to accept criticism as a trainee, but how you choose to act upon it will determine how successful you'll become.

Teachers can become set in their ways, and trainees can be a breath of fresh air in a department, with their new-fangled ideas and free lessons to prepare great resources.

Many teachers will embrace these contributions, taking copies of all your worksheets and giving you invaluable opportunities to upgrade their schemes of work to incorporate the latest literacy and numeracy strategies. After all, this will save them a week or two of getting to grips with it all over the summer.

Some teachers will be extremely wary, eyeing these methods with caution. Some departments may already use all the teaching methods you're learning about in college, and you may be lucky enough not to ever realize that some schools prefer more 'traditional' methods. However, remember that your relationship with your mentor is going to be hugely important because of the influence that person will have over your progress, even down to whether you pass, fail or quit.

To be a teacher you must have what are called 'people skills'. Getting on with your mentor could be the biggest test of this, and forcing your face into a smile from a grimace could be good preparation for everything from parents' evenings to covering drama lessons. Learn to become as organized and efficient as your mentor. Don't wait for them to ask you to prepare handouts for the next lesson, do it in advance. Don't wait for them to tell you that you're crap at handling the special needs kids, ask for advice before it comes to that – the egotistical types in particular love this. Accept the criticism and ask how you can improve. Then meet up with the other trainees from your course and compare notes about your mentors. However bad you think yours might be, there will be somebody else on your course with worse stories to tell.

If it really is getting to be an unbearable situation, talk to your course tutor. Your tutor may already be aware of problems with particular mentors. It's a sad fact that places have to be found for trainees wherever they can, and tutors don't want to jeopardize those placements by rocking the boat too much. But if you report the problems then your tutor can bear these in mind when assessing you. They might even be able to move you to a school where you can flourish without the added stresses of an unfit mentor.

And if you are a trainee and none of this applies to you, then think yourself lucky that you have an encouraging and experienced mentor!

2 Get set: Theory into practice

Firm but fair

Efficient behaviour management is the holy grail of teaching theory. It's what makes teaching so frustrating at times, and as the social issues affecting children become more complex, so the number of strategies to deal with behaviour expands, and new possibilities are created.

It's often necessary to take a look inwards at your own teaching style and assess what it is you're doing right, what could be improved, and how you can remind yourself of strategies for dealing with disruptive behaviour that have long become buried under the automated reflex to hand out detentions.

Personally, in its simplest form, I see my teaching style as being a balance between the characteristics of the two prison warders from the BBC comedy *Porridge*. Now bear with me here, and I'll explain. In the series there are two main prison warders, Fulton Mackay and Henry Barrowclough.

Mackay is the strict disciplinarian, who barks orders at the prisoners and never ever gives them the benefit of the doubt. He is always on the prowl, suspects that the men would be up to no good if he wasn't so vigilant, and that the men relish making him look foolish.

Mackay's opposite number is Barrowclough, who pussyfoots around the men, trying not to trouble the troublemakers with his orders. He takes personal advice from the prisoners, and his home life is an open book to them. He believes that a sympathetic approach will be far more useful for their rehabilitation, and of course, they mostly take absolute liberties with his good nature. However, one or two episodes show that he can still command respect, and he is liked far more than Mackay, the man who barks his orders and is wound up in return.

The secret of classroom management, I believe, is to get the balance between the Mackay side of the personality and the Barrowclough side exactly right. This stasis is rarely achieved for long, in my experience. Each day I start out probably a bit too much like Barrowclough. I might tell some of them (selectively) about my weekend when they ask during registration. I may allow myself to be diverted from my lesson plan to bring in a personal experience if it illustrates a point. I'm sympathetic, squatting down to reason quietly with the child who has just thrown all his or her books on the floor. I even let them go to the toilet if they look really desperate.

But as the day wears on, and the nagging continues, and my quiet reinforcement of rules and instructions starts to fall on deaf ears, I feel the Mackay side of my teacher self start to emerge. Requests for the toilet are scrutinized with suspicion. I squint at the child who claims his or her bladder is full, wondering if they just want to wander around the school, or perhaps flood a few sinks. I whirl round from writing on the board, hands on hips, at the slightest hint of giggling. I stop offering the choices suggested on training days, such as, 'You can choose to get on quietly with your work, or you can choose to continue throwing your pencil around, in which case there will be a consequence'. Instead I raise my voice, dole out those consequences to various corners of the classroom, and probably lose respect in doing so. But my patience is completely eroded by the time I'm asked yet again what they should do, because they weren't listening the first, second and third times.

So that's my theory, using an old and well-loved TV comedy series. Achieve the right balance between Barrowclough and Mackay, and the whole classroom discipline problem will be solved. I don't know if there are any more similarities between Slade Prison and any classroom I happen to be in, but I shall definitely be watching future re-runs of *Porridge* closely to see what other tips I can pick up for classroom management. Cheaper and more readily available than a day's in-service training, anyway.

Top tips

You don't just have to watch episodes of 1970s comedies to gain insight into classroom management. Your school should have in place some kind of system where you can observe your colleagues teaching. If this is carried out on a regular basis, rather than being a horrific once a year process filled with paranoia, it's an excellent opportunity to see how your colleagues deal with behavioural issues. It's even better if this is carried out between departments, because if you have trouble with one or two pupils in particular, you could request that you watch another teacher take that class.

You may not agree with all the tactics used by your colleagues, but something positive can come out of that too: it helps you to reflect upon your own strategies, and sharpen up some of the techniques that you use in light of what you have observed.

Preventing misbehaviour

One way to prevent misbehaviour is to anticipate it. Think of all the outside factors affecting your pupils. One of these is the weather. The following scenario might sound familiar.

It seems like a normal day, but even the best of classes are hyperactive and fussy. And the last lesson, perhaps a middling group, is the kind of fuss-fest that makes you wonder where it all went wrong. Kids are turning up late, and they all seem to be either in a strop or feeling too ill/hot/cold to do any thinking. The lesson suffers several interruptions from messengers who are probably just sent on trivial errands by teachers desperate to be rid of them from their own lessons.

Before doing anything else, check an almanac. Chances are you will have just experienced a lesson under the influence of a full moon. No, don't lock me in the funny farm yet, bear with me. Schools do seem to be affected by the weather, as well as the lunar cycle. That's not just some new age excuse, or mediaeval reasoning from the days when lunacy was blamed solely on the moon. Every teacher has experienced the tension that a rainy day brings, and it's not just down to the kids being cooped up at breaktimes.

Younger kids go mad in the playground when it's windy, charging around in circles like the autumn leaves. On a sunny summer's day the school is half empty, with an amazing bug sweeping the kids most desperate for a tan. Some teachers even break the rules and take their

classes outside to sit under a shady tree, without completing the necessary risk assessment paperwork first. They
instead weigh up the risks of a leaf falling on a child's
head against the number of migraines brought on by the
sun beating through the classroom window.

Other cycles affect how the children are going to
behave, too. How far you are into the term will affect
how the children perform. Energy levels become rapidly
depleted towards the end of term for teachers, and so too
for children. Add to this any exciting forthcoming events
or festivities, such as Christmas, and the pupils will seem
to veer dramatically between nervous energy and
complete exhaustion.

You can almost tell what week you're in by analysing
the behaviour in your classroom. In week one the kids
need easing back into work as their minds have seized up
thanks to a diet of television, texting, and video games.
Books have been lost. Homework is forgotten. The most
important thing is catching up with their mates, making
new alliances and enemies, and woe betide the teacher
that tries to encourage any independent thinking if it isn't
to do with how to beat that wretched monster on level
eight of 'Violent Shoot-'em-up in Space'.

Week two is the best week of the term. The kids are
more settled. They are even willing to learn in some
extreme cases. They have not yet got back into their
disruptive little ways, well, not much anyway. When you
first start teaching, and are given your own classes for the
first time, and you're sizing each other up, this is known
as the honeymoon period. The false sense of security and
competence almost gets you through to pay day. But not
quite. Because it's generally in the third week of term
that everything kicks off.

What happens in week three? It must be a combination

of things. I'm sure there are PhDs on the topic. Or there should be anyway. The more restless kids start remembering their favourite tricks. They get bored with actually doing homework, and instead hone their skills of excuse-making. They see if they can push it just a little further than they have ever done before. Detentions become part of the daily routine for some of them. Unless there are any important events in the school or year calendar, the rest of the weeks in any given term may well slide downhill from this point.

Top tips

It's useful to bear in mind the cycles that affect the pupils when you plan your lessons. Don't assume they will have the same concentration skills in week five as they did three weeks before. Opportunities for misbehaviour diminish if you plan well-structured lessons with a range of activities to keep them on their toes.

The other side to this is that you must keep some flexibility in your lesson plans too. Consider that even a single snowflake fluttering down outside can bring chaos to your classroom as they try to rush to the window and start chattering about being snowed in. Imagine then, how a storm or particularly rainy day will affect the moods of the children, and adjust your lesson as necessary to take into account the diversions and distractions that can be anticipated. For example, don't rely on technology if there's a storm forecast, because you may experience power cuts. If it's exceptionally sunny, find a shady spot outside where you can take them out to at least pretend to work: a nature trail or drama activity might suit here.

Most importantly, ignore outside influences at your

own peril. Incorporate them or allow for them, but be flexible too. If you anticipate that external factors may cause a problem with the behaviour of individuals or a class, you can minimize, or perhaps even prevent, opportunities for misbehaviour.

Mixed abilities

In secondary school, classes are generally taught either as mixed ability, or as ability sets. Both methods have their supporters, and are backed up with philosophies detailing why they are the best thing for the pupils.

What these generalizations often overlook, though, is the fact that within any group that is set, there are still a whole range of mixed abilities. Maybe the children all learn by different methods. Maybe they understand some things but cannot grasp others. Or maybe they just couldn't be bothered on the day they had the tests that sorted them into sets: their attainment might not be a reflection of their true ability.

All children have their own special needs, but some are categorized as such and given a little code to identify them. Special educational needs (SN or SEN) pupils broadly fall into two categories – those with emotional or behavioural difficulties, and those with learning difficulties. Some schools have a special group for the SEN pupils, while others mix them up among the teaching groups. The general trend has been towards inclusion, although there are schools admitting defeat and moving away from that policy.

Learning difficulties can be specific, such as dyslexia, or general, where a child struggles with basic literacy, for example. What can be annoying is the assumption by many staff that because a pupil has poor literacy skills, they are not capable of following a full curriculum. Many subjects are set according to exam results, but special needs kids may be in a set of their own. Fair enough, you might think, but schemes of work dictate that we should be delivering a very basic scheme to the SEN classes, assuming that because they can't write very well, then they won't be able to grasp anything else that is thrown at them.

Time and time again I have found that the SEN classes I teach have lively, inquisitive and enthusiastic kids. They are being marked down because of their inability to construct grammatically correct sentences, but their subject knowledge can be absolutely amazing. In fact, it can outstrip the knowledge and understanding of lower and middle sets. Should a pupil be denied access to develop a full range of skills because they can't write without an assistant to help them?

With lower sets, the pupils are generally there because either their behaviour is so bad that they never bother trying to achieve good marks, or they do try hard but their brain power is limited. Of course, I realize that bad behaviour often arises when a pupil is disaffected because they don't understand what's going on, but the wily ones are those with a spark of intelligence, because they work out the ways to really wind up their teachers.

Lessons with bottom sets often follow familiar patterns. Trying to encourage the pupils to draw conclusions about anything, or remember a few key facts from lesson to lesson, is excruciating. You can see the pain of concentration in their scrunched up faces, and you start to wish that there was an easy access starter motor for their brains. Their thought processes are all over the place. They can't concentrate. But my point is, if I put the kids from the SEN class head to head in a panel quiz with a lower set group, the SEN class would whip their butts. And yet which group gets the wordsearches and colouring in projects? You guessed it, that's a SEN speciality.

Top tips

If you teach lower sets, try out some of the SEN resources with them. Very often the game playing and colouring in of pictures will engage them more than sticking rigidly to the department's scheme of work. Surely it's better that they learn a few facts and skills than none at all, because the normal curriculum may well be beyond them.

Mixed ability teaching can be a challenge for the teacher, and a lot more work. But it's also useful practice to get into the habit of differentiating work, because you often need to do this in groups that are set anyway. The theories on the best way to teach mixed abilities abound. You could split them into groups or teams of approximately the same ability. Or you could ensure that each group has a stronger member and a weaker member, a loud pupil and one of the quieter kids, and so on. Make sure that in group work each member of the group has a job to do, such as reporting back to the class or taking notes. Make sure everyone has a go at all of these jobs. Variety is the best way to keep pupils engaged and on task. Changing activities every ten to fifteen minutes keeps the pupils interested, and it also motivates those who find one particular activity a struggle.

With mixed ability groups, there will be pupils who finish before all the rest. This could be because they have rushed their work, and it's not of a sufficient standard. If they are this impatient, they will require a further activity that reinforces what they have just done, rather than being told to check their work or redraft it.

Other pupils finish quickly and proudly show you the thorough work they have completed; these pupils require extension work to stretch them and help them access higher skills and grades. If the same pupil continually finishes the work well ahead of schedule, you may consider setting them some project work that they can get on with while the rest of the class catch up. The nature of the project work will depend on the subject you teach, but there are many resources out there in government documents and on websites for gifted and talented pupils, so somebody in your department should know about these already.

Even if your school sets pupils for lessons, you should constantly be aware that there are still a wide range of abilities in that room at any one time. Children with poor literacy skills may still have the cognitive powers to excel at activities that don't involve writing, whereas others may cruise along in an attempt to get away with doing the minimum work possible. Your responsibility as a teacher is to the individuals in that class, and as such you must ensure that your lesson stretches all of them in some way.

Impressing the inspectors

As I write, the inspection process is changing (yet again), but whatever effect this has on the school as a whole, you know that your role will pretty much stay the same.

Firstly comes the panic. And it's there to stay. Heads of departments flap around looking for something called the department handbook, and then discover it masquerading as a tatty red folder at the back of the stock cupboard. Even worse, it seems to be full of schemes of work that bear no relation to what is currently taught, and have nothing to do with the current National Curriculum. This means a rewrite is in order, and the canniest of heads of departments will delegate this job to the newest member of staff, who is more likely to remember what they were taught on their teacher training course.

It's not just schemes of work that worries departments though, but also the vagueness of the policies and procedures bit. Does constantly hearing the pupils cry, 'This is boring' count as self-assessment? Is sending the naughtiest child on errands around the school for the whole lesson really the most effective way of dealing with behavioural issues, and if so, should it be noted in the procedures folder? Will anybody notice the correlation between the neatest wall displays in the school and the most incompetent teachers?

Knowing that an inspection is imminent means that a large number of meetings will be called, all of which do nothing to settle general staff nerves, and most of which state the obvious in several different ways. Reams of paperwork are distributed, some of which will be the lesson plan sheets you'll need to fill in for every lesson you teach for the duration of the inspectors' visit, just in case they surprise you with an observation.

Once all the paperwork has been completed, and the children briefed on how to behave and bribed to wear the proper school uniform, and the corridors have been cleaned like never before, a strange calm descends on the place. During the week of inspection, there's nothing left to do but wait. Wait to be asked questions that the headteacher has already answered on your behalf. Wait to see if the slowly turning handle on the classroom door is an inspector or just a late-comer. Wait to have the sum of all your teaching expertise, form filling, behaviour management, and projected ethos reduced to just one word, be it good or satisfactory or something better or worse.

Top tips

This is something I overheard in a staffroom, and I must admit I haven't yet tried it out. When you have inspectors in your classroom, train the children beforehand in this little technique. A question to the class should have one of two reactions. Firstly, a raised right hand means that they know the answer. Secondly, a raised left hand means that they don't know the answer. Result: a sea of raised hands to every question posed to the class. The only problem I can forsee is with those not so bright sparks who need help distinguishing between left and right. Or you could just do what some of the less inspired teachers in one school I taught in did, which was to deliver a lesson in front of the inspectors that they had already taught the week beforehand, which ensured the kids knew what they were doing.

Seriously, though, if you are a good teacher, it will shine through. And even if you're not graded the way you think you deserve, at least for next time you can show how much you've improved. Inspections are a bit like horoscopes anyway: if they are good, you want to believe them, and if they are disappointing, you can always pour scorn on the whole thing.

Encourage other staff (or student teachers if that idea is too nerve-wracking) to observe your lessons frequently.

This will help you to get used to having somebody else in your lesson, and you should also get into the habit of delivering the type of lesson an inspector would want to see. Make sure you have clear lesson objectives, and that these are made explicit to the pupils. Don't ignore the importance of a plenary, either.

Keep the pupils' books marked up to date, and if your department doesn't have a policy on self-assessment, initiate one yourself. This could be a sheet of tick boxes that the pupils fill in to assess how they are doing with regards to the subject requirements, completing homework, and so on. Make sure they are also aware of what grade they are working at, whether this is a National Curriculum level in Key Stage 3 or potential GCSE grade. They should also be aware of what they could do to improve their grade. You could display the criteria on your classroom wall, along with some examples of work at the different grades. Make sure that each pupil has one or two targets to work on each half term to improve their work, and that they record the homework that you set (even if they don't do it).

Keep on top of your paperwork. Get into the habit of keeping a record of the lessons you have planned even if your school doesn't provide you with the necessary forms. One school I worked in insisted each teacher hand in their planning folder to the headteacher once every half term. This folder showed the lesson plan in three or four bullet points, and there was also room for a comment on how the lesson went. I used the space to jot down the names of any pupil causing a major problem because of their behaviour, and also where the next lesson needed to pick up from. This way, the headteacher could compare planning files and see who the real troublemakers were. If you keep your records up to date on a lesson by lesson basis, or even on a daily basis, the task doesn't become overwhelming, and it's an easy habit to get into.

Hoard your records at the end of each term and year. Don't throw away registers or mark books until six years have lapsed, just to be on the safe side. It's not just inspectors that may require to see these documents, but also your own school's management team, perhaps when you go begging for a management point or some other pay rise.

3 Go: The art of teaching

The lesson introduction

The lesson introduction really consists of two parts: getting the pupils into the classroom in the first place, and then getting them settled enough to focus on the subject matter of the day.

Advice on the topic normally states that you should conduct this process in a firm business-like manner, but one which lets the pupils feel welcomed into the room. Ideally, the pupils should line up neatly and quietly outside the classroom, and when they are ready the teacher should lead them in, perhaps standing at the door with a welcoming smile, and remind them of what they need to do: take coats off, get books out, sit quietly, and so on.

After this perfect start, the pupils are then ready to start the lesson with all the correct equipment out in front of them, and the teacher firmly in charge. There are a number of ways you can start a lesson, such as a quick-fire question and answer session about the previous lesson, explaining how this lesson will fit into what they have been studying, or a warm-up activity.

I think we would all love to be able to start our lessons like this. I have been in schools where this does indeed happen, and while the pupils are the normal rabble in the playground at breaktime, once they are in a lesson they know what is expected of them. Sadly, though, however optimistic your expectations are, the start of your lesson may sound more like a typical example from my day.

It's the first lesson of the day. There are 22 pupils present when they have all finally drifted in from assembly or form registration, or whatever Year 8 have been up to for the first half hour of school. For two of them it would seem to be smoking, because they come in reeking of fags. The ideal scenario of the class lining up outside until they are settled, and then being led into the room by me is not a policy the architecture of the school building would support. The corridors would start to resemble an M25 gridlock if pupils had to line up outside, with streams of kids bashing past them with their huge bags and dangerous elbows.

There would have been one more pupil present but he broke his behaviour contract two seconds after entering the room. His long-suffering LSA (learning support assistant) shepherded him out of the room as I tried to ignore the tipping over of chairs and punches thrown everywhere. It's a great distraction for the rest of the group so I try to carry on normally. There are a few kids in the school on behaviour contracts. It's what happens when the kid should really be excluded for a culmination of major incidents, but the governing body or the local authority or the law disagrees, and forces the headteacher and staff to carry on with the kid in the school.

So far, the first five minutes of my lesson have consisted of a handful of children turning up on time, sitting there quietly with their things in front of them while waiting for everybody else to arrive. Others have drifted in, fussing over bags and being reminded several times to get out their pens. Several children have dozily wandered into the wrong classroom or cheekily stuck their heads round the door to yell a greeting to one of their friends, before legging it down the corridor. And of course that one pupil has already been taken out by his LSA, just as all the kids were starting to settle.

So that's the first part of my lesson introduction: I've managed to get the correct pupils into the classroom, sat in the right seats, with their bags under the table and their coats and baseball caps removed. But I haven't quite finished: there are still some sitting there without the right equipment in front of them. It then takes another five minutes of fussing to locate books for those who haven't left them at home, dish out scrap paper for those who forgot or lost their books, and find pens for everyone. I shouldn't be amazed that kids still come to school with no pens, but I can't believe it happens so often.

It's ten minutes into the lesson by now. One way to remind the class of what we did last lesson, and how this will lead into today's lesson, is to go over any homework they have been set. Homework is usually set to reinforce what has been covered in the lesson, or to provide extension work to stretch the pupils. To be honest, I rarely set this group homework. It never gets done, so I can't rely on work being completed for following lessons. If they can't bring in their own pens and books, they sure aren't going to get homework organized. Still, it's an experiment I try out every now and again to see if there's any improvement. In addition, the school insists I set homework according to a timetable, and sometimes even audits the type of homework I set over a term, along with completion rates.

The homework experiment from last week failed, because none of them completed the simple task of illustrating the cover of their new project booklets. If anyone asks, the learning objective of this homework is to select suitable illustrations, therefore demonstrating their ability to identify the key points of the project. I thought they would enjoy the colouring in aspect the most.

But, in fact, only four of them have even brought in their booklets. Three others were absent when the homework was set, which means that I must have a homework completion rate of ... ooh, it must be just 85 per cent for this group. I note the figure down on my register and hear the headteacher's words ringing in my ears, 'Let's all aim for a 100 per cent homework completion rate! I won't settle for less than 90 per cent!' I'd settle for one of the group doing something, but I know it's not to be.

As three pupils were absent last lesson, I have to rapidly think of a way to summarize an hour's lesson from a week ago to bring them up to speed. It turns out to be a beneficial exercise because a sea of gormless faces stare blankly back when I ask some simple questions based on last week's lesson. We look back at the text books and I desperately search for any flickers of recognition as we scan the pictures in the book. Finally, one pupil manages to answer a simple question and I feel we are able to move on to the topic of today's lesson.

Top tips

There's the theory of efficient teaching, and then there's the practice, and at times there is a huge gulf between the two. However, even when you feel the forces are conspiring against you; with children let out of previous lessons early or late, sent on errands when they should be in your lesson, given every opportunity to drift the corridors rather than line up outside your room, don't give up. There are still some principles and routines you can keep in place, and hopefully drill into pupils arriving at your lessons. It may take some time, especially when other teachers don't insist on such standards, but eventually the penny will drop and you should see a more efficient start to your lessons in time.

Pupils should all know where their seats are in the room. If you teach the class across several different rooms with different seating plans this is more difficult, but don't allow the pupils to swap seats. At the beginning of the year you may have asked them to sit in alphabetical order, or a boy–girl combination, or provided them with a seating plan they should stick to.

With younger groups, having some kind of team incentive will encourage groups of pupils to settle. You could divide the class into five or six groups depending on where they sit, and allocate points on how well the groups enter the classroom, or to the first group sitting there ready with all their equipment out, and even for their performance in team quizzes. Keep score of how well they do, and make sure there is some incentive at the end of the half term or whole term, using your school's reward system or small prizes for the winning team. Pupils will soon realize if one member of their team is continually letting them down, and some pupils respond better to the cajoling of their peers than to what sounds like the teacher's constant nagging.

Have an introductory activity that can be started by those pupils who do arrive on time, something which will keep them occupied while you deal with the latecomers and the inevitable fussing they bring. The type of activity will depend on the subject, but it could be a quick quiz they can work through at their own pace, or thinking of five key points from the previous lesson. Once everybody is present, feedback from this type of task should provide a reminder to the class, and a summary for any pupils who were absent last lesson. Writing the instructions on the board will save you from feeling like a parrot if the pupils drift into the lesson at different times.

Even if your lessons aren't allowed the chances you think they deserve, there are still ways to salvage the routine and stop the chaos at the first possible opportunity.

The lesson in progress

No matter how long your lesson lasts, from a 40 minute session to a two hour double lesson, you have to visualize your time in segments. There's the lesson introduction, usually taking the first five or ten minutes. At the end, there's the lesson plenary, which must be juggled with the separate activity of packing away: again, usually allow five or ten minutes.

The rest of your lesson will ideally consist of a balance of well-paced activities, incorporating individual, pair and group work. It will be a mixture of whole class teaching and smaller group activities, giving the teacher a chance to make their way around the classroom and speak to each child at least once during the lesson, ensuring that the child has understood and is following the learning objectives. What? What's that? Are you sniggering at the back? This comes highly recommended, you know. It's what we expect of every lesson from every teacher, isn't it?

Every now and again I like to stop and do some basic

arithmetic with my classes. Not because I'm consciously incorporating numeracy across the curriculum (although now it's been mentioned, that's not a bad way of doing it), but because I like to show them how much time is wasted by the class as a whole, and by certain members of the class.

If I give them ten minutes to complete an activity, I remind them of when half their time has gone. I'll warn them when there's a minute left. Then I'll ask them to be quiet so we can have some feedback. And I'll wait. Sometimes I'll repeat the instruction. Sometimes I'll make over-exaggerated glances at my watch, cross my arms and sigh loudly. If things don't improve, I turn around, write on the board 'Time wasted' and then make a big deal of looking at my watch, hovering by the board to write down a figure showing the number of minutes elapsed. Eventually, they shut up. By this time, two or three minutes could have passed since my first request for quiet.

This is when I like to do my mental arithmetic. If we have three ten minute activities and I have to wait for three minutes at the end of each one, how long have I waited for? Now subtract your total from the length, in minutes, that breaktime lasts ... they soon get the message.

But there are individuals, too, who repeatedly waste lesson time and distract the majority of the pupils. It's all very well to punish them by keeping them behind or following the school's discipline procedure, but nothing is going to regain those lost minutes for the rest of the class. The amount of fussing that goes on is incredible. Here is an example of a typical exchange that follows even the simplest of instructions, a fuss created by four or five children:

Me: Right, copy the title from the board into your exercise book.

Pupils: What? I don't get it.

Me: What do you mean, you don't get it? All you're doing is copying the title from the board.

Pupils: What's the title?

   What are we doing?

   He's taken my pen.

   Can I have some paper?

Me: Where's your book?

Pupils: You've lost it.

Me: *I've* lost it? How could that be?

Pupils: What's the title?

   Can I borrow a pen?

Me: Okay, when you've copied down the title, put down your pen so I can see you're ready.

Pupils: I haven't got a pen.

Me: Well use a pencil.

Pupils: I haven't got a pencil.

   Miss, he's taken my book.

Me: Right, stop talking please.

   I'm still waiting for you to stop talking.

   Michael, sit down. Tina, turn around.

Pupils: What are we doing?

Me: I'm waiting for you to stop talking so I can explain to everyone what we're going to do.

Silence for a millisecond

Me: Last lesson we found out what a glacier is. Who can remind us?

Pupils: What does glacier mean?

Me: That's what I'm asking you! Look it up in your glossary, you wrote the meaning down last lesson.

Pupils: Where? I can't remember.

Get off my book!

It's a lump of ice!

Me: Okay ... So who can remember how glaciers are formed?

Pupils: In the fridge.

Me: No, and please don't shout out.

Pupils: Erm ...

Me: Right then, let's remind ourselves by looking in the books at the last thing you wrote.

Pupils: What, the title?

Miss, he's got my pen.

Shut up, David.

Why are we studying glaciers? It's booooring.

Me: *spontaneously combusts*

And all this is without the irritating interruptions that I comment upon elsewhere.

Top tips

Pace and timing are vitally important during your lesson. Spend too long on one activity and the class will begin to drift off, go off task, doodle on the desks and possibly each other. Each chunk of the lesson should be building towards the main learning objective, whatever that may be and however you get there: by role-play, comprehension questions, filling in diagrams, and so on.

During the lesson, there are advantages to be gained by circulating the room. Behaviour management experts will often tell you to scan the class, circulate the room, and make eye contact, so you may think of yourself as a lion on the prowl rather than a teacher. This is something an inspector would expect to see you carrying out, and it has definite uses as well. During group work you will often realize the pupils are like animatronics, those robotic puppets that only jump into action when stimulated by an approaching audience. It's only when you patrol your classroom that you realize that half of each group will be asleep on the desk, and the other half will be talking about completely irrelevant gossip. The first pupil to spot the teacher's approach will usually announce something relevant in a loud voice, so that the rest of the group spring into action too.

You should have extension work that builds on that work for those who finish early. Some pupils will rush through their work and do not complete it to a very high standard. For these, they require extension work that consolidates the skills they have been working on. Other pupils finish the original work to a very high standard well within the time given, and for these you should provide work which allows them to develop their skills further and which moves them on to the next level.

With extension work, pupils don't like to feel they're being punished by being given extra work just for finishing early. To combat this, you might like to try a variation of the 'traffic light system' of work. With any piece of work, let all the children see all the possible work to be completed. Grade the absolute minimum amount you would expect with the colour red. Tell them that everybody must finish the red work in the allotted time, or they will be expected to finish it at break or lunchtime. The next lot of work can be graded as amber. This is the section that you expect almost everybody to have finished in the time, although there may be two or three weaker pupils who don't manage it. The final section is the extension work, which you grade as green.

Planning the timing of your lesson is all very well, but

another key word here is flexibility. Most of the time you will have to make allowances during the lesson to deal with unacceptable behaviour, an inability to listen, and interruptions from outside. It's far better to ensure that all the pupils have understood one or two topics thoroughly than to race through three of them so quickly that nobody is quite sure what they are supposed to have learned.

The lesson plenary

The lesson plenary is a fancy way of saying the end or completion of the lesson, and contrary to popular belief and practice, it should not be the manic five minutes at the end where you suddenly remember to set the homework, collect in the equipment, and pack away.

Even if your classroom has no clock, the pupils will take their cues from the shuffling noises and scraping chairs in neighbouring classrooms as a sign to pack away, and it's not such a surprising sight to turn around from writing the summarizing sentence on the board to see the pupils sitting there with bare desks, and wearing coats, baseball caps, and the occasional personal stereo. If this is the case, you have some serious training to do with your classes. Once again, they are revealing an insight into how your colleagues treat the plenary of their lessons, and you have to show the pupils that your expectations are different to this.

There are certain things that need to be done during any one lesson: collecting in equipment, setting homework, breathing a sigh of relief. But most importantly, you need to make sure that your pupils are well aware of what they should have learned that lesson, by reinforcing the key learning objectives. In other words, summarize what you've covered. This is especially important if you've been subjected to several irritating interruptions, and found yourself stopping and starting to deal with an unruly pupil or two.

Top tips

Packing away can be a struggle on its own. Sometimes, convincing the more light-fingered members of the class to relinquish their bounty of glue and colouring pencils that you distributed earlier will take some time. You have more of a negotiating angle if your lesson is just before a break, because you can keep the class back until these things are returned. Put one of the most popular pupils in charge of collecting in the right amount of equipment if you suspect it could disappear, and you could get a better result than standing there with hands on hips a minute after the bell, the next class waiting to come in, and no real leg to stand on. Make sure you don't need superfluous stationery during your lesson plenary, and get it collected in before you start to summarize the lesson.

As for homework, it shouldn't be an after-thought or add-on to the lesson. Set the homework at the beginning of the lesson. Make sure each pupil writes down the instructions and the date it is due in. Tell them to write it down even if they don't understand what it's about at that stage, and assure them that they will know what to do by the end of the lesson. Towards the end of the lesson, review the homework task again to ensure everybody understands it, and leave yourself time for further explanation if necessary.

I have experimented with setting the homework in the second half of the lesson, but many pupils are so used to having homework set right at the end, that they take this ritual as their cue to pack away, until you point out that there are still twenty minutes left of the lesson.

Timing is one of the most important aspects to any lesson. It's easy for time to slip away if you have to deal with behavioural issues, and you try to race through the second topic you wanted to cover that period. But you may as well consider it a waste of a lesson if you do not summarize or reinforce what the pupils should have learned by the end. This gives you a chance to check that they have understood the key points. The plenary may take many forms, depending on the nature of the subject that you teach.

It could be that you have introduced several new key terms and want to ensure the pupils understand what they mean. In this case your plenary could consist of asking pairs to produce a one sentence summary of each key term, then choosing a good example of each to write up on the board, and for the pupils to copy into their exercise books. You could briefly state what you're going to do next lesson, so that the pupils see how the topics all fit together. If the lesson has been heavily factual, your plenary could be a question and answer session. This can be light-hearted in form, for example a team quiz with the winning team being allowed to leave for break first.

Irritating interruptions

In any one lesson, you may have achieved what you thought was hardly possible at the start: the class are settled, they all have something to write with and to write on (excluding the desk), most of the text books are turned to the right pages, and they are focused on the task, and even engaged in the lesson. It's one of those sparkly magic moments in teaching when you can barely believe that this was the same rabble that sauntered in twenty minutes ago, and you gaze around the classroom with a mixture of awe, amazement, and the feeling that you're walking on eggshells.

Then it happens. Your peace is shattered. Above the murmuring of the busy bees hard at work can be heard a sharp knock at the door. You pause for a moment, wondering if there is genuinely somebody there or if it's just corridor wanderers having a laugh, but before you can scoot over to the door to open it, in barge two girls, who announce loudly that the music teacher would like to see all choir members at lunchtime. Too late. The magical working atmosphere has been destroyed, and before you have time to admonish the girls, they have started up a conversation with one of their friends across the room, before disappearing to interrupt the next class.

The next set of interruptions may come from the PE department, who have taken advantage of the three boys without their kit and sent them on a message to collect names for all those attending athletics trials at the weekend. Or to remind the football players of the practice at lunchtime. Or to borrow trainers from their friends who just happen to be in your class.

But that's not all! Expect to be interrupted by pupils asking to borrow your stapler, enquiring if you have any spare exercise books, collecting leftover dinner money for charity, brandishing sponsor forms, wanting to use your computer to print off their homework, looking for spare chairs or board rubbers or plain paper. They might want to search the room because they are sure they left their pencil case here last lesson. Further pupils may bring you notes from other teachers, forms to fill in right there and then, telephone messages, requests from the deputy head to see a certain pupil right at that moment, or report cards left behind by a pupil during their previous lesson.

Pupils on messages don't seem to notice if your class are straining to hear a class member reading slowly from the text book, or if the group at the front are giving their presentation to the class. Unless you are quick enough to catch the messenger's gaze and perform an exaggerated 'shhhh' sign, they will start to read aloud their note as quickly as possible, probably with the nerves associated with barging into a different year group's lesson.

Then there are the movements in and out of the room by pupils with sports matches to attend, instrument lessons, appointments with the headteacher following an incident at lunchtime, report cards left with the previous teacher, dentist appointments, nosebleeds and desperate toilet visits, and so on.

Colleagues may disturb you in full flow to retrieve something they left in your room when they were teaching there earlier, or to get something from the stock cupboard, or to ask your opinion about a pupil whose parents they are meeting after school.

It's bad enough that your own class members can provide plenty of their own irritating interruptions, but these ones seem beyond your control. Is there any solution beyond keeping sentry by your classroom door for the entire lesson, blocking any messenger from barging in, or glowering with disapproval?

Top tips

Very often, it's tempting to blame the pupil for interrupting your lesson, and mostly their manner can leave a lot to be desired. But most times the pupil is only there because a colleague has told them to deliver a message, or given them permission to leave their lesson. Sometimes, it's very tempting to get rid of your most annoying pupil by sending them on an errand. Here's a tip I was given for doing just that: keep a brown envelope containing a blank piece of paper inside it ready at all times. With the permission of several of your colleagues, write their names on the front of the envelope. When you have reached the end of your tether, give the envelope to the irritating kid and tell him to take it to each of the teachers named on the front and ask them to tick their name when they've read it.

When your colleagues receive the envelope they will understand the need to delay this child for as long as possible, so will usually say, 'Wait there a minute. I haven't time to read it just yet'. After at least five minutes have passed the teacher pretends to read the contents of the envelope, ticks their name, and the kid goes on to the next member of staff.

It's not something I've practised, as there seem to be enough children milling around the school corridors when they should be in lessons, and I'm afraid that one day they might just all gang together and start plotting the ultimate in lesson interruptions. We already have enough rogue fire alarms and flooded toilets, and I shudder to think what's next.

This is a whole-school issue that needs to be enforced from the top downwards. If that isn't happening, there are certain things you can do in the way of damage limitation. If the class are working happily, intercept each messenger before they get the chance to disturb the positive working atmosphere. Make a note of what they want, then send them on their way. You can deliver the message to the class in your own time, or single out the child that is needed with minimum fuss and embarrassment to the pupil concerned. If the pupil messengers are selling raffle tickets or collecting for charity, send them away and tell them to come back five minutes before the bell. Chances are that they will forget or by that time be too concerned with dashing back to their original classrooms to grab their own bags.

Handling irritating interruptions to your lesson is another example of how it is possible to maintain your own standards when all around you are losing theirs. Just remember that it works both ways. Only let pupils out of your classroom when absolutely necessary, and if you stop disturbing your colleagues with requests for stationery when they are trying to deliver a lesson or keep a lid on an unruly class, they might just stop disturbing you too.

Learning support assistants

Picture the scene. The pupils are sitting attentively for once and awaiting the fantastic lesson you are about to deliver. But hang on! There's some talking going on at the back! You're just about to open your mouth and chastise the talker when you notice that it's not one of the pupils at all, but the learning support assistant (LSA) who is with one of the pupils this lesson. Do you ask her to please stop talking? Do you announce a general warning to the class to be quiet? Or do you try to ignore it, hoping that she's really explaining some work when deep down you know that she's gossiping in a completely irrelevant way?

LSAs are a tricky addition to your classroom. There are

many completely professional LSAs, who take their jobs very seriously and are an asset to the classroom. They may be in the class to support one or more children with learning difficulties, or they may have been assigned to assist the class in general if there are a number of weak members. They may accompany a particular pupil to all subjects, or the LSAs may concentrate on particular subjects, becoming experts in one or two subjects and gaining an enviable insight into a range of teaching styles. You might also know them as teaching assistants (TAs).

LSAs are not there to gossip with the children. I also believe that it's not in their job remit to encourage the kids to ignore the teacher, to shout at the class when they believe it's too noisy, to colour in their planners, to ignore explanations of activities that they are supposed to be helping the pupils with, to check their mobiles for text messages, or to type up worksheets on the class computer while their charge struggles or gives up altogether and starts flicking ink around the room. But it does, unfortunately, happen.

Understandably, it's not easy for the LSAs. The money and conditions are rubbish, for a start. Many of them are paid by the hour, the hourly rate is low, and the work is during term time only. Each teacher will vary in their expectations of the LSA, and it can be difficult to listen to instructions while trying to prevent the pupil doing whatever naughty deed they are desperately attempting.

There are some schools whose army of LSAs work with complete efficiency. They have regular meetings, are given time to collect schemes of work in advance and read worksheets and handouts prior to the lesson. If you speak with them during the lesson to tell them what you will be doing next time, they take it all on board, and may even have suggestions for particular resources that their charges may require. They listen, they give enough help to let their charge complete the work, but they don't do the work for them in exchange for an easy life. These LSAs are also few and far between.

If the organization and training of LSAs in your school is not sufficient, then you can only expect a group of LSAs who are not quite sure what their specific roles are, and they quickly settle into being a passive member of the class, especially if they are never told what they should be doing. Just like a bored pupil, many LSAs can become a disruption in their own way.

Top tips

OK, so unfortunately at your school the LSAs don't receive enough training or instruction in their duties, and they think that getting on with kids means chatting away during your lesson. You have to become proactive here, not just for your own peace of mind, but also because if the LSA is not doing the job properly, there's at least one child in that class who will suffer as a result.

Find out who the LSA is supporting, and sit them by that pupil. Just like the rest of the class, make sure they always have a specific spot to sit in. Near the front of the room is best, because it's easier to get their attention. Some pupils are teased about having an LSA, but you don't have to be explicit about who they are there to help. There are teachers who like to have the LSA sat at the back of the classroom, to pick up on any naughtiness going on, but this can be distracting for them.

If you have a couple of minutes at the beginning of the lesson, show the LSA any materials you'll be giving out that lesson, and explain briefly what the main tasks will be. Although they are usually the best raiders of the locked stationery cupboard that I have ever come across, make sure they have all the equipment they will need for the lesson.

The frown of non-comprehension on an LSA's face when you are explaining something to the class is a good indicator of how clear your instructions are. Once the pupils are working on their own, make sure that the LSA, as well as the children, is on the right track. Again, if there is time at the end of the lesson, as the pupils are packing away, give the LSA copies of the work you'll be doing next lesson. Sometimes they pretend to look interested, and sometimes they even take the handouts with them, but as long as you remember to thank them after each lesson, you'll know you've done your best to help the LSA to help the pupils.

Incorporating ICT

When it comes to information and communications technology (ICT) there are certain teachers who have all the necessary gadgets to guarantee the kids come flocking to their lessons with tails wagging excitedly – OK, of course I exaggerate – but these teachers have things I covet, and it fills me with envy. Need to show a video? Pah! These teachers consign videos to museums – it's *so* 1980s, darling. Instead, they slip a DVD into their laptop, power up the interactive whiteboard (or the second-rate option, focus the projector), and skip straight past the rude bits in *Romeo and Juliet* without the kids trying to get a glimpse of bare breast in fast motion.

Or what better way to engage the kids in a lesson than by getting them to make their own slides for a presentation? Why risk scissors and glue and all the fussing and potential finger-sticking and eye-poking when 'cut and paste' is a phrase only to be applied to finding pictures from the internet to add to an online project? Perhaps subject knowledge can be reinforced by playing one of the BBC's excellent online games, or by explaining it to an email pen pal?

Oh yes, ICT is a wonderful thing. I know, I've been a fan since my first click into the world of the Internet about a decade ago; I know how to incorporate ICT into my lessons and I've got the pieces of paper to prove it. Actually, come to think of it, I never did receive anything to prove I completed my New Opportunities Fund training, but then again, I don't think that particular piece of paper would be worth anything anyway.

I'm the kind of teacher that used to grab the ICT supplements from the paper with great enthusiasm, filing useful articles in the appropriate places in my schemes of work, and bookmarking useful websites with obsessive fervour. But these days I can't bear to flick through any more articles featuring smiling teachers photographed against a background of a suite of state of the art computers, scanners and printers. I feel like they're gloating at me, just like the teachers at school who swan about with laptops. What I really don't need is yet another bright spark telling me how I could use this or that to enhance my teaching. I feel like I'm stuck in the Dark Ages, because I've been forgotten in this ICT revolution. The classroom next door requires sunglasses to walk past the open door, lest the glare of the interactive whiteboard dazzle me into spontaneous technology worship, while I make do with a solitary PC, un-networked and quite frankly, pretty much unloved.

There must be teachers out there who would love to

have a PC in the classroom, and who could tell me of the thousand ways I could incorporate it into my every lesson. I know, alright. I'm just not happy about it. It gets used – and then it crashes. I try to love it, I honestly do, but children fighting over the use of the PC is just one more hassle I could do without. Do you know how many lessons it would take to let every child in the class have their turn on the PC?

On top of that, there's the pupil's perspective. Once they've been dazzled by the truly multi-media experience of Mrs Flash next door with her all-singing, all-dancing, all-working PCs, why should they be pacified with the promise of a five minute blast on a PC that takes ten minutes to whirr into action? In fact, why should they sit still for even five minutes and squint at my diagrams etched onto the blackboard? Well, they don't. I fear that their experience in my lessons will taint their view of the subject, and they will forever associate it with chalk dust particles floating in the rays of brilliant light that beam through from next door.

Top tips

We're all supposed to be at it now. ICT is a key skill that should be incorporated into every scheme of work, and put into action by every teacher, congenital Luddite or not. Of course, one of the big problems with this is access to the necessary equipment. I know there are many teachers who breathe a sigh of relief when the ICT budget doesn't stretch as far as their corner of the school, but believe me, ICT is a truly wonderful thing and can be used in so many ways. Even if you don't know how to get onto the Internet, if a colleague recommends a website that can be used for research, just supply the pupils with the address and they will be away. It may well be the same content that is contained in those dusty old text books, but it will probably be presented in an alternative way, with games, quizzes, interactive diagrams and animation that will reinforce their learning.

The pupils will probably know how to word process and use spreadsheets and the Internet from IT lessons, and even if this is at a basic level there are ways of incorporating this into your lessons. Drafting and redrafting work is a much easier task on a PC, particularly for those who struggle with their handwriting and despise all the mistakes they seem to constantly make.

Some teachers are worried by computers because they don't have much expertise themselves. Let me reassure you: whenever I can get near the computer suite I usually learn something new from the pupils. With ICT, your role as a teacher changes. You are no longer there to deliver information, but rather to enable them to learn. And by showing you how to do something, the pupils are demonstrating their competence in a key skill. With ICT the teacher doesn't have to appear omniscient, and even though it helps to have some know-how of the software packages you're using, there will usually be some techno-whizz in the class who is more than willing to show off their abilities.

Now all you need is access to the ICT equipment in the first place ... !

Incorporating communication skills

There seem to be enough demands in the curriculum already, but every subject has to consider the key skill of literacy, also known in a slightly different way as communication. And rightly so, too. It's what teachers have been doing for years anyway: correcting spellings, adding missing punctuation, groaning in despair at the incomprehensible mess they are wasting a perfectly good Sunday afternoon trying to decipher.

Pupils should know about Standard English, and when they are expected to use it. Text message abbreviations are not, as far as I'm aware, yet considered to be Standard English, but this doesn't stop even the more able pupil from using it in their GCSE coursework.

Skills such as letter writing can seem antiquated to the children, who have grown up with email and text messaging. Need to write a letter of complaint? Email the company. Want to send a postcard from holiday? Text messaging is quicker than working out the local phrase for 'Two stamps please'. Pen pal? What's that? There's nothing exotic any longer about communicating with somebody from a different culture; some kids do it every night in chat rooms on the Internet. Thank you letters? They just use their mobiles to call or text. Email seems a better way of saying thank you, especially when it takes no time at all to attach a digital photograph of yourself wearing that lovely new knitted jumper.

Even though many companies are moving towards online recruitment, there are still many who prefer correspondence by post. Granny may not know how to operate email or a mobile. Isn't there still something special about receiving a brightly coloured postcard through the letterbox and admiring the glamorous stamp? There are many reasons why traditional writing skills are still important, and schools may just be the last bastions in which to teach and instil these skills. Literacy should include knowing when and how to use different forms of communication. Different subjects may favour specific forms, such as report writing and the use of the passive phrase in science, or essay writing in history, but the school as a whole should ensure that no form is neglected.

Top tips

Holding up a united front is what can win the battle, and this applies to tackling literacy as a whole-school issue. One way of doing this is by concentrating on one particular aspect of writing across the whole school in any one week of term. So, for example, for the first week back pupils are told to concentrate on using capital letters in the right places, whether they are in English or science, maths or geography. For the second week of term, the emphasis is on writing in paragraphs, and the third week could be making sure commas are used correctly. Laminated notices could be distributed to each classroom on a Friday afternoon to be displayed for the following week, as a constant reminder of what that week's focus is. When teachers are marking work produced that week, they should look out for how well the pupil has used that week's literacy focus.

Another technique to improve literacy is a focus on spellings by each department. A list of key spellings for each year group is drawn up, and then given to the pupils to stick into their exercise books so that they have it there as a constant reference. They should also attempt to learn the spellings, and this is where form teachers can help too. If each form teacher has the appropriate sets of spellings from every subject for their year group, they can run spelling tests once a week, or whenever there's a spare ten minutes.

Literacy and communication are not just about spellings and sentence structure, but many of the other aspects are already incorporated into each department's schemes of work. Pupils should be given opportunities to present findings to the class and to take part in discussions, so that they are confident in their speaking and listening skills too. It's the listening part that many of them have exceptional difficulty with. During oral work, be forceful about penalizing pupils who don't listen to what others have to say, which you can do by deducting marks from their work. By reinforcing crucial skills, such as how to sit still and show you are listening to somebody else, across the subject spectrum, the majority of pupils can learn by habit and repetition what is expected of them.

4 Children can be the most irritating things

Playing truant

Some schools have community police constables to sweep the local shopping centres, bus shelters, parks and other hangouts to find errant children who really should be knuckling down to double maths instead of kicking tin cans around and defacing public buildings with badly spelt graffiti. Other schools employ an administrative officer to ring or even text message the parents of absent kids. Some local authorities have successfully prosecuted parents who allow their children to play hookie from school.

But let's look at this from another perspective. Let's leave aside the fact that the missing kids could be exposed to as much danger hanging around parks/shopping centres/abandoned buildings during school hours as they are at weekends and evenings. Let's just imagine the relief on the teacher's face when they are told by the class that so-and-so is absent today, and therefore won't be there to call out, disrupt the lesson, annoy the other children, throw their book on the floor, swear, refuse to do any work, claim to have no writing implements, and carry out the familiar rituals of the child who doesn't want to be in school. And then ask yourself: who is really losing out if this child chooses to be absent?

It would be great if it was as simple as that. However, we all know that truanting children only add to the chaos. Firstly, there may well be the five minutes of tale-telling from other class members, particularly if it's only your lesson that the pupil is skipping. Then you are obliged to follow school procedures, whether that be a note to reception or the head of year, or a phone call to a specified member of staff.

If the pupil is dragged back into your lesson halfway through from behind the bike sheds, this causes disruption. Whether the pupil misses half a lesson or a week's worth, once they are seated back in your room they will demand more attention simply because they don't know what they've missed and will need help to catch up. This is karma payback for the serene feeling of being secretly glad that your most disruptive pupil was playing hookie.

Top tips

Make the most of the lessons where certain children are missing, but remember that, theoretically, they will have to catch up when they do attend the lesson, which can be a disruption in itself. Whatever their reasons are for missing the lessons, assume that it is because there is something stressful going on in their lives elsewhere.

At the end of the lesson, borrow the exercise book of a conscientious pupil so that you can photocopy the work they have done. When the truant does return, they can be given the photocopy at the beginning of the lesson to read through as you begin your recap from last lesson.

Or, for the more dedicated teacher, tap into the motivational powers of information technology, and add your lesson notes to the school intranet so that all absentees can have access to key notes or the work they have missed. Scanning a kid's work takes about the same time and effort as photocopying it, and can have a positive effect on the pupil who donated their work to this good cause. You could even use this as a motivational technique for those pupils who are in the lesson, encouraging them to produce neat, tidy and, most importantly, legible work.

Language matters

Let me get this clear from the start: I'm not averse to a bit of strong language. Everyone has their own opinions on swearing. Some find it disrespectful and offensive. Others regard it as a sign that the user has a limited vocabulary. I don't know quite how this argument would go. Just have the thesaurus handy next time you bang your elbow on a door handle or drop a pile of neatly stacked and sorted worksheets. Others are eager to reclaim the words from our Anglo-Saxon heritage, and can quote every example of Chaucer's fruity choice of words, most of which would be worth a 50p contribution to any office's swear box.

Personally, I find that there are some situations where nothing says it quite like a swear word. Go on, choose one and say it now. Listen to the way it bursts from the mouth and rolls off the tongue. It's a little explosion of a sound that stops internal combustion in times of stress. But let me get this straight ... I would *never* swear in the classroom, which, at times, takes all the self-restraint I possess. In fact, being a frequent swearer, one of the most difficult obstacles I had to overcome when I first started teaching was to eliminate such words from my conversations, which meant that I mostly spoke very slowly at first, sieving the words as they tried to tumble off my tongue.

I soon learned some substitution techniques. 'For goodness sake' was my watered down version of something far stronger, 'Oh dear' replaced another curse, and so on. But something that I'm still perplexed about is where to draw the line. TV companies and radio stations have their own lists of prohibited and restricted words, which include words that can be used in rationed amounts. But it seems in schools there are no hard and fast rules.

There are so many different situations where swearing is a potential or actual problem. Kids who grow up with families that swear all the time are immune to its power to shock, and use swear words in their conversations too. Other kids are well aware of the power of the four letter word, and try it out with their mates in the corridors and playground. Where should a teacher draw the line? Many will remind children in their class about choosing suitable language for a situation, unless the swear word is directed at the teacher as an insult. Others, often weary and battle-worn, have learned the art of 'see no evil, hear no evil' and close their ears and eyes to anything happening in corridors and the back corner of the classroom that is not affecting them personally.

One teacher I worked with would scream in a child's face about 'the language of the gutter' if she heard them utter anything she found offensive. In my own classroom, I chastised a member of my class who said that something was 'crap'. I asked them to choose another word instead, and when they questioned why, I told them that they should answer without swearing. The pupil was genuinely confused by this. 'But crap isn't a swear word,' was the reply. 'Mr S (the PE teacher) calls us crap all the time.'

So here lies the problem. Which words should be on the banned list for classrooms, and even corridors? There are some obvious candidates, but also more and more words, like 'crap', are slipping into a murky grey area. Time and time again, teachers are reminded that rule setting has to be a fair process. Most classrooms have a set of rules displayed on the wall so that the pupils know what is expected of them. After all, you can't win the game if you don't know the rules. But would a sign saying 'Use suitable language' be too vague?

Meanwhile, after a day of minding my own language, the expletives jostle for space as soon as I leave the school grounds, particularly during my drive home, should some git try to cut me up. Swear words can take the place of nouns, verbs, adjectives and adverbs. Versatile little things. That's the power of language.

Top tips

Ensure you have your own rules about using suitable language in the classroom. Very often the pupils will try to shock you, or try things out to see how much they can get away with. If your school has no clear or defined policy on this matter, it's even more important that you have your own.

Carry on being consistent in the corridors, playground and canteen. There's no point in laying down the law in your classroom if you allow pupils to swear within your earshot elsewhere in the school.

Don't over-react to swearing, though. Some pupils

grow up surrounded by this kind of language, and don't realize that it can cause offence. They soon will if you make a huge fuss, though. Help them to expand their vocabulary by displaying lists of suitable adjectives on the wall that they could use instead of saying that something's 'crap'. Use a thesaurus to investigate alternative words. This is an activity you could do together with your class, depending on the age group and subject you teach.

Pupils who swear in anger, especially if accompanied by the slamming the desk, knocking over the chair and storming out of the room routine, should be dealt with in the usual manner that your school discipline policy has set out.

It's important to remember, though, that not all swearing is done as a form of aggression, so incidents should only be punished if the intention was to cause offence. Otherwise, it's time to do your job as educator – and re-educate those foul mouths!

Well versed in the art of lying

Are kids really so lazy at home? Or so naïvely stupid? Do they think that hiding the scrap paper or rubbish on their chair rather than walking the four steps to the bin to throw it away won't be found out? That even though they sit in the same seat every lesson, I won't know who is responsible? Ditto for the wall display vandalism, and the thickest crime of all, writing on the desk where they sit, especially when accompanied by their own name or initials. I remember being far more cunning about these things at school. Have kids lost the initiative, or just the intelligence?

Similarly there are the cases of leaving their own,

named exercise book on the desk because they couldn't be bothered to hand it to the collector-in, and then subsequently couldn't be bothered to put it in the pile in the cupboard.

Parents, if your child claims they have looked everywhere for their book, they are most probably lying. If they say the teacher has got it, they are most probably lying. The truth is, the teacher has either had to tidy it away for them, in the general skivvy session that is necessary between classes, or the teacher has thrown it in the bin to serve the lazy git right. Besides, then there's less marking.

Talking of lying, kids do it a lot. Of course, teachers do it sometimes too, but only when it's for the best, for example to the questions 'Have you marked our books yet?' and 'Why are the computers still broken?', and it's almost compulsory in job interviews, especially to the question 'Why do you want this promotion, with its associated pay rise?'

But one of the most annoying things about working with kids is the bare-faced blatant lies they tell you all day long, and even worse is that they think they have pulled the wool over your eyes. Fact is, kids, we know you are lying to us. Yes you were chewing gum, no you haven't swallowed it, no you haven't done your homework, no your dog didn't eat it, yes you did write on the desk, yes you were hitting each other, no you haven't lost your tie/shoes/book, yes you did swear, no you don't have an excuse for being late, et bloody cetera. Lies, lies and damned lies.

There's just nothing we can do about it. Really. Our hands are tied. And sometimes it's just not worth the challenge. Your word against ours. But it all gets stored up, and one day, revenge will be very sweet ... if I ever work out how exactly I can get my own back and prove that you never actually did get one over on your teacher.

Top tips

Kids are going to lie to you. There's no getting around that fact. The best way to cope is not to take it personally. Lying is an automated defence mechanism, clicking into place when they realize they are wrong and can see no way of wriggling out of it. What you as the teacher should ask yourself is, what do you want the result of this situation to be? To avoid being wound up, make sure your instructions are clear, and reiterate them frequently.

If it's the old chestnut of failing to hand in homework for whatever fanciful reason the pupil comes up with, you need to ensure that you follow your school's policy on homework submission. Insist that any failure to submit homework by the deadline must be accompanied by a note from the parent. This won't always work with every child. Sometimes they don't see their parent in time because they are a shift-worker, for example. Give the pupil a second deadline, usually next lesson, and ensure they make a note of this. If you establish a routine, the pupil knows where they stand, and what the consequences of failure are. Some pupils simply don't have a quiet space at home to do their homework, or have a mass of obligations, from caring for a sick parent or large family, to a constant round of music practices and swimming lessons. If you establish a routine of setting homework on a certain day and expecting it in after a reasonable period, not just the day after, most pupils will get to grips with this.

Make sure the homework task is interesting. Set something that will appeal to their creativity or curiosity. Writing up notes or finishing questions started in class are not the most scintillating of tasks. Remember why homework is set in the first place: it's not a punishment (although you may feel differently when marking it!). A primary aim of homework is to check the pupil's knowledge and understanding of what they have learnt in lessons. You could ask them to present the key points of what they have learnt in a different format, such as an explanation for a younger pupil or a poster. You could make it into a challenge or quest, and focus on the work of pupils who do submit their work on time by showing it in lessons, displaying it on the walls, and rewarding those pupils who hand in decent work on time if your school has a reward system in place. Try to eliminate the reasons why a pupil is disinclined to produce good quality homework for you. For older pupils, the nature of coursework should be an incentive in itself, but again there may be a multitude of reasons why the pupil cannot work to a deadline. The answer may be as simple as offering them a quiet place to work on it during lunchtimes, or breaking tasks down into smaller, more manageable, chunks.

These tips are not foolproof, but could reduce the number of times you hear the phrase 'Our printer's out of ink' in any one day. You can also try to have an answer for each excuse. Their printer may well be out of ink, so lend the pupil a floppy disk and let them print the work out in school.

Lies often come as an answer to questions. Don't give the child an opportunity to lie by resisting asking them questions when you know what the answer will be. Don't ask, 'Are you chewing?' Give the pupil an immediate choice: they must come and put their gum in the bin or they will lose their breaktime. Don't ask them what they are up to, tell them you know what they are up to (some bluff may be required here) and that if they don't cease that behaviour then they will face the consequence of their actions.

Consistency is the key here. Make sure the class knows that writing on the desk will result in a shift of desk cleaning at lunchtime. Point out to them that you know who sits where, and what lessons you have had that day. Sometimes the pupils genuinely don't realize how easy it is to solve their crime, and you need to make it clear that they won't get away with it. If you try to limit their opportunities to lie to you, this could well have a knock-on effect in your ability to manage their behaviour too.

Classroom banter

Eavesdropping on kids' conversations can be one of the perks of the job. Granted, most of the kids talk about pretty mindless stuff most of the time, but at times it's hard to suppress a giggle, smirk or sigh at some of their claptrap.

It also reminds you that although drugs and sex references litter their conversations, they still have much to learn, and sometimes it's easy to assume that they know more than they actually do. While a class of 12 year olds will happily discuss the merits of bongs and skunk, only one will be able to explain to the rest what a joyrider or jaywalker is.

Meanwhile, the street insults rebound around the room with wild abandon, so I'm cheerfully informed of which pupils have a 'ho' for a mother, and who is 'so gay' – the general term of abuse, referring to anything that's bad or wrong. For example: 'Homework? That's so gay.'

Another form of eavesdropping is the ancient practice of note interception. It's an invaluable way of finding out who smokes, who's a bitch, who's going out with who, who likes who, and more seriously, who's being bullied.

I haven't had any good notes recently, either to read out to the class, or to threaten to show parents at parents' evening. I blame new technology. One of my pupils recently let slip that many of them have their mobiles switched on to 'silent' in lessons so they can text friends in other classes. How am I supposed to find out their gossip now?

Confiscating mobile phones is a grey area and it's easier to turn a blind eye than risk having something so expensive stolen from my desk. Although the one time I did confiscate a phone I was quite disappointed. I asked the pupil to show me what she had been texting in class, but she had obviously got to the delete button in time to save herself. Most of the messages were from the girl's mother, sent the previous evening, telling her to come downstairs because her dinner was ready.

Top tips

As with swearing, make it clear what language is acceptable in your classroom. Whatever the current vogue for language is, if the language could be offensive to another person, it shouldn't be used. It's a fine line to tread though: tip-toeing around certain words and phrases only makes it all the more delicious to your pupils. Sometimes the pupils use the latest slang with no real understanding of the word, so demystify it for them. A dull three minutes on its etymology will take the shine off a phrase you don't want to hear.

Mobile phones are a tricky area. They shouldn't be: in an ideal school, there would be a strict policy regarding their use. Some schools don't allow them, but if this is the rule then they must make some provision for pupils who carry them at their parents' insistence. In other schools the rules are more hazy: pupils may have phones, but they must be switched off in lessons. There will always be something distracting for pupils to fiddle about with under the desk, from passing notes and swapping football stickers, to things that don't bear thinking about. Mobile phones are just the latest distraction. If you pace about your classroom as the lesson takes place, popping up behind pupils with unnerving frequency, you will have a better chance of them keeping distractions stuffed in their bags than if you teach from the front of your classroom like a preacher on the pulpit.

Some teachers insist on silence during their lessons in a bid to stop the classroom banter, but that's an unobtainable aspiration in most subjects, particularly those that require frequent group work, or even the sharing of text books. Banter can help you to get to know your pupils better, but make sure you let your pupils know that you have the power of super hearing, and can pounce on any conversation at any time.

5 In addition to teaching

Form time

Part of the duties of most teachers will be to have a form group. The extent of the responsibilities that this entails varies enormously from school to school, as do expectations of how far your responsibility to these children stretches.

Some schools adopt the system that you start off with a bunch of fresh-faced Year 7 pupils and stay with them through the teenage traumas and tantrums until you end up with the same group in Year 11, the fresh-faced part becoming replaced by acne and thick layers of make-up.

Other schools randomly allocate their teachers with different form groups each year, while others expect teachers to stay with the same year group or key stage.

Each year group has its particular challenges, from helping new pupils find their way around a dauntingly large school building when they first start, to encouraging GCSE revision and career choices. Along the way there are a multitude of issues to deal with, from bullying and discipline to changes in family circumstances, friendships, and hormones.

Having consistency as a form group is beneficial to the

children, especially as they struggle to adapt to the new regime in secondary school of moving from lesson to lesson with different teachers. As a teacher, you get to see the group of children change and develop over the year, or even over five years. It's also often the only way you ever get to hear what's really going on in the school, either from the kids telling you about the really massive fight that occurred at lunchtime, or by the newsletters that appear in the register. No registration duty means you don't get to see what's been stuffed into the register that day, and so could end up oblivious to the fact that the following day is Sports Day, or that the whole of Year 9 are out on a trip.

At the beginning of each morning and afternoon session, form groups usually return to their form rooms to be registered. Often, the morning session is the longer of the two. Some days you might have assembly. Other days might have specific duties for the form teacher to perform, for example checking the pupils' planners or running a pastoral session. Pastoral in this case is nothing to do with scenes of rolling fields, gamboling lambs and tranquillity. It's more often than not a session the children are hardly awake for, and the teacher half stumbles through, having been handed the appropriate scheme of work by the head of year just the afternoon before. This can also be known as PSHE or a variation thereof, which stands for Personal, Social and Health Education.

As such, the pastoral session will often find the teacher making excuses about their personal smoking and drinking habits if the subject is the dangers of smoking or alcohol. You might well be cringing as you carry out the session on personal hygiene, knowing that the infamous Year 9 pupil, 'Smelly Harris', is sitting a little too close for comfort. The names of sexually transmitted diseases are seen as an opportunity to provide an anagram quiz rather than dwell on questions you really don't know the answers to, and can't seem to find in the book. Of course, you could always revert to the Internet if you have a networked computer in your classroom, but you shudder when you think of the computer technician having a laugh about your latest web search, and then not wishing to use the same toilet as you at breaktime.

The extent to which you get involved in the children's welfare will depend upon your school's policy. Some schools see your role as form tutor being to take the register and keep the kids quiet if they don't have assembly that day. Others expect your role to involve contacting parents, dealing with the latest misdemeanours of the pupils on report, chasing up homework that a colleague has mentioned to you in the staffroom, and helping to sort out the personal problems of form members.

Sometimes though, it's just you and your form for half an hour. You've taken the register. You've told them to get out their reading books or planners, or learn some spellings, while you have to distribute letters, read and reply to several letters from parents, chase up absence notes and outstanding library books, inform them of room changes and timetable changes, ensure the special needs children have written everything down correctly, collect in reply slips and money for their next trip, hunt down spare copies of letters home for children who have lost theirs – and suddenly the bell goes, and they're off, leaving you standing there waving the register as the register monitor disappears into the sea of pupils in the corridor outside.

It is better to be busy though. Having the form group for half an hour when the register took two minutes to get through can be a pain. With one ear you listen sympathetically to the pupil in tears because the dog ate their homework or their best friend called them fat, and with the other ear you hear the ever-growing crescendo in volume of pupils relishing this half hour of freedom to gossip, bang the tables, cram sweets into their mouths when they think you're not looking, and copy their best friend's homework.

Top tips

Sometimes a form group and its associated responsibilities can seem overwhelming. As with any job that seems too large, delegate. Even Year 11 pupils can be persuaded to take on 'monitor' jobs if you tell them it will go on their personal statement and impress future employers – even if none of us actually know an employer who took on a school leaver for their ability to carry a register over to reception. Appoint monitors to tidy text books, make sure the computers are switched on, ensure there is enough paper in the printer, check desks for new graffiti, close or open windows, order your lunch from the canteen – whatever you think is appropriate and makes life a little easier for you.

Getting to know the kids well over a number of years is all well and good, but they will see you as being on their side and some will begin to take liberties with regards to wearing trainers, jewellery, make-up and piercings. So much so that it's quite normal to think of yourself as a perpetual nag, one who struggles to find answers to the injustices of being a teenager, such as to why one girl is allowed to have so many piercings, even though we can't see them, and being told to pick on her instead of badgering another about his hair dye.

Keeping the pupils occupied during form periods is a critical role. They will become more resistant to this as they grow older, because they will want to spend the time discussing among themselves how drunk they got at the weekend, or why their band is going to make it big, or what a slag so-an-so is, but if you get them into a routine early on, they will know what to expect, and what your expectations are.

On days that are not assigned to assembly or PSHE sessions, plan activities that every pupil can participate in. During their first couple of years in the school, you can give them mental arithmetic tests on one day of the week, and spelling tests on another. Ask your colleagues in different departments for their lists of key spellings they expect the children to learn, and this way you can vary the spellings each week. You could have general knowledge quizzes, or quizzes on current affairs.

Another thing you could do with your form, if your head of year agrees, is to encourage them to write in personal diaries. Tell them that you are the only one who will be reading it, so if there's anything worrying them they can write it in their diary. It will help you to sort out any potential bullying issues or problems that are affecting their school work. Otherwise, the diaries can be used to write about what they did at the weekend, and this way you get to know your form members a little better.

A final idea is project work with your form. This will keep them focused, while working in groups is a tick in the citizenship box, and it even has learning objectives. A project could be something like the desert island project. Each session, the groups have to come up with part of a story depending on the information you give them. For example, in the first session you could tell them that they wake to find themselves on the beach of a desert island. They have to construct the scenario of how they got there, perhaps by a shipwreck. In the next session they have to describe day one on the island, and you can give them criteria such as describing how they make a shelter, what items they find in their pockets, where they locate food and water. This project can run and run, because you can extend it to cover as many days on the island as you choose before they are rescued, with something different to think about each day, such as drawing a map of their island, designing a raft out of certain materials, dealing with wild animals, deciding how to signal for help. Their project work could take the form of diary entries, messages in bottles, plans, designs and maps.

Being a form tutor can be a challenging position because of the multitude of responsibilities to perform each week. Sometimes the most challenging thing can be keeping the form occupied with something constructive while you deal with pupils on an individual basis. Project work is an ideal way to do this.

Covering for a colleague

An inevitable part of the job, and one of the most frustrating, is covering for a colleague. It's an issue that we can't be too sanctimonious about, because there are times when our own lessons need covering, but being told that you have lost your non-contact time, in which you were planning to catch up with some marking or photocopying, in order to sit in with the naughtiest group in Year 9, is guaranteed to make your heart sink.

There are several whinges that can be heard about covering for colleagues. One of these is getting to the classroom and finding that no work has been set by your colleague. But for me, number one rant is the *word-search*. I really hate wordsearches. Nothing against the literary form, as I extend this revulsion of the 'search' type puzzle to those deviants involving numbers, musical notes, chemical equations and so on, *ad infinitum*.

It's the sinking feeling I experience every time I spot the freshly photocopied stack of mindless teasers. Sorry, tormentors. You'd think that I'd be grateful that work had been set. So why do I despise these stalwarts of the cover lesson? Well, let me explain.

Firstly, there are many teachers who believe that a word/number/symbol search will last every pupil the whole hour. They obviously take the associated origami session into account too, also known as making paper aeroplanes and testing their flying capabilities in restricted spaces.

Secondly, but not separately: these puzzles are not a bit of light relief or an easy lesson for the pupil and teacher; they are dull as particularly dank dishwater. While there are some devotees, the majority of the pupils greet these 'treats' with groans and an immense amount of fussing over highlighter pens – yep, even Year 10s.

Thirdly, I would like to ask: of what educational value are wordsearches? Some might say that they help with literacy, especially now it's expected in all areas of the curriculum, but that is poor justification in my humble opinion. It may only be a cover lesson, but I still have the same desires: I want lessons with learning outcomes and interested children. The emphasis is on the last two words of that sentence. While some teachers see cover lessons as 'keeping a lid on it' or 'babysitting services', I find that having the pupils completing a task makes the session whizz past quicker for all concerned.

Besides, I'd like to see the inspector's face the day an observed teacher announces to the class: 'By the end of this lesson, you will have filled in a wordsearch after carefully selecting the correct colour of highlighter pen and resisting the primal urge to fold the paper into aeroplanes.'

Top tips

There are two sides to the tips for this problem. One is your duty to a colleague that has to cover a lesson for you, and the other is your duty when covering.

Let's face it, we all want an easy life. Some teachers will take this too literally. They stroll into the cover lesson, stack of marking under their arm, holler at the class to sit down and shut up, and proceed to do their utmost to ignore the chaos around them as they apply red marks to the books in front of them. The kids might be initially excited by a free lesson, but boredom soon sets in. And there always seems to be one studious pupil sitting in the corner, trying to complete some homework amidst the din. Even if the absent teacher has set work, it's ignored, with the cover teacher now seeming like the good guy for letting the class off the work.

This isn't the easy life. Give the pupils something to do and they might well call out in protest, but they will be far more settled with something to occupy them. This may seem obvious, but there seem to be teachers out there who have forgotten this fact. Even if you know nothing about the subject, you can set a task that will have an outcome. Ask them to prepare twenty questions on their current topic of work, with answers. When they have finished this, and you have got at least some of your work done if you still insist, collect in their work and finish off with a team quiz based on what they have produced during the lesson.

As for setting work for your own cover lesson, make sure it is something your colleague will thank you for. They will undoubtedly be after a quiet lesson, so set work that the pupils can progress through individually, without the need to hunt round the room for equipment they don't have, like colouring pencils or rulers. Leave plenty of paper, and ensure your instructions ask for the work to be collected in at the end of the lesson. Your instructions should also be extremely clear, and indicate where books and paper can be found. Make sure you set enough work, with an enjoyable extension activity that comes as a reward to the children that complete it, not as a punishment of more repetitive work.

Don't use this as an opportunity to introduce a new topic, and don't expect to follow straight on from the lesson when you next see the class. Allow for absences, idleness, and a colleague who might prefer to ignore the work altogether while the pupils set about demolishing the wall displays.

The school production

Whether the school production is an annual music and dance extravaganza or a nativity play of a familiar format, its existence takes priority over everything else. It is usually referred to as a 'production' rather than a play or musical, perhaps because the latter terms promise something so specific, which a 'production' doesn't necessarily have to deliver.

The school production becomes a black hole into which the children get sucked, swiftly followed by lesson plans, lunch breaks, and sanity. The theory goes that the more children there are taking part, then the more relatives there will be to fill up the school hall when the production is finally staged. The flip-side of this is that the more children are involved, the more disruptive it is for everyone else.

As a rule, teachers take one of two sides. There are those that sign up to help, relishing the opportunity to be a part of something that lets them see a different side to the children, to do something as a team, and to create something of which the school can be proud.

The other side is those that abstain. Abstention may seem like the lazy option, but it is in fact the martyr's role. Sometimes there simply is no role for you, as a teacher, to fulfil. This is particularly true when you join a new school. It matters not if you have previously single-handedly designed costumes for a whole stable of nativity animals or coordinated the lighting and special effects for *Oliver!*, because there will usually be some old codger of a teacher who has done that job since time began and sticks to it tenaciously, growling slightly at anyone who threatens the existing hierarchy.

Even worse, teachers not involved in the production end up babysitting all the children too naughty or disaffected to take part, and this is the reason that so many teachers sign up to help in the first place.

Of those volunteering their assistance, a good many just want to be in charge. It's not just the children who have stars in their eyes, but also the drama teacher. The art department's contribution to scenery painting is not a selfless act of philanthropy, but probably their greatest chance for a wide audience for their work. It's also penance for the lack of marking that comes with that particular job.

If, as a parent, your kids are in a school production this year, and you're nodding off between the scenes in which they feature, here's a little game for you. Count how many teachers you can see spaced around the hall and at the edge of the stage, and then rank them in order of starry-eyed desperation. You can award them points if they are mouthing the words to the songs, distracting the performers on stage by pointing out directions, or just generally trying to look important. Then try to spot your child's teacher(s). If they are absent, it will be because they have had a rough time containing the excluded kids, or are at that moment calming down the over-excited lambs backstage, and will never see the production themselves. So give them a sympathetic smile at the next parents' evening, and say no more about it . . .

Top tips

Find yourself a niche when it comes to helping with the school production. Drama, art and music teachers have particular roles to play, and if you teach design and technology you should be able to contribute in some important way. If you don't want to be assigned to 'crowd control' or any of the other less desirable jobs, you have to be quick off the mark to sign up for something more fulfilling. In addition, by getting more involved you could earn brownie points from the senior management, plus you can understand why the kids are hyperactive or haven't done their homework by the time they get to your lesson.

If you're flexible, you could incorporate aspects of the production into your lessons to motivate the pupils in between rehearsals. Science teachers could take the opportunity to explain how the lighting works. In maths, ask the children to find out the optimal ticket price to offset overheads and make a small profit. Geographers could find out something about the place where the play is supposed to be set, or complete a project on entertainment facilities in the locality. Historians may be able to investigate the period in which the play was set or written, whether focusing on the politics of the time or even the fashions, which could then inform the art department and those designing the costumes. In English, pupils could study advertising materials for shows and plays, and then create their own. Or they could try turning some of the script into prose, perhaps trying to change the genre.

There are many possibilities for incorporating the production into lessons, and by doing so you will hopefully keep the pupils interested in learning even when there's chaos in other parts of the school day. If you know that various members of your classes will be missing lessons, you could set project work so that the children can pick up what they were doing even if they miss a lesson or two. Or you could make sure that each lesson, while following the same theme, is a self-contained lesson that doesn't require any knowledge from the last in order for the pupils to participate.

Training courses

Training courses are an essential part of teachers' working lives. Also known as Inset (in-service training), you will spend a few days each year in school without the pupils there, so that you can be brought up to date on new school initiatives, or participate in first aid training, or doodle on your notepad as a speaker enlightens you about something that you apparently need to know. A day in school without the kids sounds great until you suddenly begin to sympathize with their daily plight of having to sit still for hours on end and listen carefully in case something really important is being said. Some Inset sessions take place in 'twilight' time, which is after school hours. It is aptly named, as after a hard day's teaching, this part of the day can be particularly tiring, and can be akin to the twilight zone. You may or may not turn into a zombie.

Then there are courses that mean you get a day off school with the promise of coffee breaks and buffet lunches. As a teacher, you will be sent on a course for one of a few reasons. Maybe the government has introduced a new strategy that you must learn about, digest and implement by Monday week, and so off you go to learn about it in some third rate hotel in the back of beyond for the day.

Or it could be that your school throws a load of brochures your way and tells you to take your pick from the courses, as they've discovered you haven't been on a course for over three years, and are worried that this must be affecting the way you teach – perhaps manifesting itself in that grimace every time you have to cover for colleagues who are on yet another course.

For paranoid teachers, being told you are to attend a course on behaviour management, for example, is a huge blow to the ego, and will lead to many accusing stares at fellow members of staff as you think about why you're the only one who needs help with their behaviour management. You may also silently accuse colleagues of grassing you up to the Inset coordinator because your classes are always so noisy.

Training courses themselves take on such variety, but here I want to demonstrate what training courses aim to do, and how this affects the mind of an average teacher.

The last training course I was sent on was on behaviour management (see my paranoid points above), which accounts for at least half of all training courses I reckon, being the issue that will never be resolved in teaching, however many government initiatives are issued, and however many psychologists spend their careers trying to find new solutions to ancient problems. I could sum up all those training courses in one sentence: kids have been, and will always be, kids, so accept it.

These courses on behaviour management, of which I have experienced a fair few in my time, are not really designed to give you any new and all-encompassing strategies that really work in the classroom, because if it was that simple, I'm sure the inventor or discoverer would sell the secret to a publishing company for multi-millions rather than trekking round the guest lecturer circuit in beige slacks and an ill-matching tie-and-jacket combo. (Training courses leave plenty of time to analyse the clothing choices of the speakers.)

Instead, many training courses trot out the Child Psychology 101 course, in the hope that it will change the way that you, the teacher, feels about children – understanding why they swear at you, ignore you, lie to you, and so on – so that you don't become angry with them, but instead reach a state of pure enlightenment with the class from hell.

This brainwashing effect will work to varying degrees for a limited period after the training course only, depending on how desperate you are to believe it. For example, a couple of the key messages I took with me from my last course were as follows.

First, don't tell children what to do. They won't do it. Instead give them choices, for example: 'Either you choose to put that away, or you choose to continue waving it around the room, in which case there will be a consequence. It's your choice.' I must admit, my mind boggles once I get onto the next stage in this imaginary scenario, for example: 'You can choose to remove your hands from my neck, or you can choose to (cough) carry on and face the (choke) consequence.'

Second, bad behaviour that follows such a statement should be ignored as much as possible. No child wishes to lose face in front of their friends, so they will swear, raise their eyes to the heavens, badmouth you, etc. You, the teacher, should remain focused on the outcome you want, rather than the route the child takes in achieving it. On no account swear back, or tell them that they won't be at school for ever, and you know where they live.

But let me put this into context for you, and show you how training courses can allow your brain to accept that you are entirely helpless and unable to administer the punishment the child deserves, while neutralizing all urges to show the child how much they have wound you up.

The other day I was pulling out of the school gates when I saw a bad-ass 12-year-old pupil messing about in the road. He was pushing one of the other kids into the road, and then kicking the tyres of parked cars, spitting at windscreens, and ignoring the fact that the road is always a vehicular minefield of double-parked parents, and teachers with their feet on the accelerator. I checked my mirrors, and there was no other teacher around to deal with it, or not, as the case may be. As I saw a bus coming down that side of the road, I acted instinctively. Well, that's not strictly true. I'm afraid if I dig deep enough, my instinct is a dark one indeed – I would have been quite happy for that little git to reap the consequences of his actions, whatever they may be when he was stood in the middle of the road with a bus approaching.

Instead, my civil response was to beep my horn, wind down my window and call over to him to get out of the road. As I wound up my window, I heard him turn to his friends and say something along the lines of, 'No I will not f★★★★★★ get out of the f★★★★★★ road', and I'm sure I would have seen the appropriate hand gestures had I glanced back.

So what would your response be? With me, at first, pre-training course teacher emerged. This involved much muttering under my breath, listing ways I could get the sod back the next day, and fervent wishes that he experienced firsthand the consequences of his bloody actions.

Then I checked my rear view mirror. He was no longer in the middle of the road, but was hopping down the side, one leg on the pavement and one in the gutter. And then the effects of the training course began to kick in. I felt a calmness wash over me, with all thoughts of revenge being washed away and replaced by a feeling of peace, and probably some glib phrase like 'kids will be kids'.

You see, he *had* followed my instructions – almost – and got out of the road. The secondary bad behaviour was merely his way of not losing face in front of the others. It can't have been directed at me, his saviour and moral guardian. What he really wanted to say was, 'Thank you, I have been behaving foolishly, I will take your advice because I know you are right and that under your stern and nagging exterior you are doing these things because you really care'.

And so my evening wasn't ruined by thinking that a little idiot had got the better of me. The training course worked! I'm brainwashed! I then had to try to block out the thought that all those psychologists are far more successful with adult behaviour patterns than the behaviour of children . . .

Top tips

Training courses might seem to consist of teaching the proverbial grandmother how to suck eggs, but there's always something there you can take away with you. Whether that something is new strategies to try out in the classroom or the free biros and notepads given to delegates will depend on the quality of the course.

Courses can remind you of all those different tactics you used to try but have since forgotten. Attending a course with teachers from different schools gives you a chance to swap notes on everything from whole-school policies to how many lessons they spend on a particular part of the curriculum. Networking with other teachers is useful in so many ways, and not just so you have somebody to play 'keyword bingo' with at the next course you attend.

Holidays

Sometimes, when I've had a bad day, I ask myself, or anyone vaguely in the vicinity, why I'm a teacher. One of the replies I hear most often is, 'Oh well, just think of the holidays'. It's true, of course, that the long breaks teachers get make the job seem very attractive. Sometimes each half term presents itself not as a chunk of weeks or a scheme of work, but as days to be counted down to when I don't have to get up so early, and can stay up a bit later on a week night.

But as any teacher will quickly point out, we need the holidays. Not just to recover from an exhausting job, both physically and mentally, because there are many other professions whose hours exceed any European recommendations, and which have their own particular stresses. The holidays are, admittedly, a chance to catch up with everything for which there aren't enough hours in the week during term time. There is always something hanging over you as a teacher, whether it's marking or planning or even extra research into your own subject area.

I have now concluded, after many experiments, that the only way for me as a teacher to enjoy the school holidays is to get away. I'm not talking about jetting off to foreign places as soon as the final bell rings, although of course that is one option that I would love to take. A few days in a different environment is enough to recharge the batteries, however exhausting it turns out to be.

That way, I'm not tempted to sit at my computer surfing the net under the guise of research or work, discovering that there are a thousand different ways to teach one particular lesson, which ultimately makes me feel inadequate and not at all refreshed. And then of course I end up trying to buy some work related books online and get caught up in the online retailers' snares of special offers and free postage and packaging if I spend just a little bit more, and before I know it I'm checking out the top 100 paperbacks and wishing I had more time to read for pleasure ... if only I didn't spend so long online ...

Discussion boards for teachers are also quite compulsive, especially if I post a response, because I then feel compelled to check the site every hour just to see if somebody's responded to my post, and then I wander off onto threads that are completely irrelevant but sometimes entertaining, mainly comparing how many reports have been written and who has the worst deal when it comes to work that must be completed during the holidays.

Nope, get away from the computer and the teetering piles of unmarked books is my answer. Being in a different place means that time takes on a different meaning too. The twilight time of the end of the school day becomes time for a late lunch. I no longer feel compelled to get ready for bed before the BBC's *News at 10*. I still wake up early of course, but this is a bonus, because it means more time to spend doing different things.

It's the delight in the small things that makes a difference. Meandering along in the car, stopping wherever I fancy, not just doggedly driving from home to school and back again. Going to see a film in the afternoon, in a cinema devoid of children because they are all queuing to see the latest hyped-up blockbuster. I can even visit a tourist attraction and enjoy it, without getting the urge to count heads or tell a child to remove their fingers from one of the exhibits, although I must confess the gift shop always makes a profit out of me when I spot anything vaguely educational.

But then it's back home, noticing afresh that the house-work needs doing, reports need writing, and that there are only a couple of days left before the holiday is officially over. And of course I haven't checked my email or the discussion boards so there goes an afternoon (or two) sat in front of the computer, urging myself to clear the desk space to make room for the school work, but not being able to let go just yet ...

One thing I never do, though, is go near the school

building during the holidays. This is particularly true for the summer break. I know that there are tortured souls who spend the first week or two of the summer holidays faithfully going into school to clear out filing cabinets, plan for next term, and so on. They often then take a week or two off before starting up again with the unnecessary going-into-school thing, to prepare for the next term (AGAIN?!) and be there for exam results.

I tend to think of this as a boy scout attitude of do-gooding, but in all seriousness there is something immensely sad about the whole thing. I suspect that the teachers who inhabit the empty corridors and echoing classrooms in holiday time either have no lives of their own, or perhaps hate their families so much that they would rather be in a stuffy old building during the best time of the year.

I really am struggling to discover what takes up so much time though. What takes up to four weeks to do that can't be crammed into the Inset day at the start of term? I imagine it to be a coffee-swilling dithering and gossiping kind of work. By the end of the summer term, books are all marked, the first week's lessons should only consist of the introductory kind, there's no work yet to stick up on the walls ... what are they doing? When you start a new job, you're normally sent your timetable over the summer and expected in at school on the first day of term. There's not much you can do to prepare until school gets under way. That's not to say I don't have my own lists of things to do, but I wouldn't waste my precious time off worrying over them. The summer holidays are really the only holidays where teachers can feel a small sense of completion.

Let's face it, we were given a long holiday for a reason. We need to be refreshed, we need to bring something extra and fun back to the classroom when we finally have to drag ourselves back, and we're not going to get that by hanging around a grim old building all summer, seeing the same grey faces of our colleagues and whinging about work. So make the most of it, and my advice to teachers who find themselves chained to their blackboards is: go home! Leave it all behind!

Top tips

As a teacher, there are certain things you have to accept. One of them is that however long you spend changing fonts on your worksheets for Year 8 to make them more appealing, they are still going to graffiti all over them and leave them on your floor at the end of the lesson. Sometimes the pressure and volume of work can seem overwhelming. There are always things that can be improved, cupboards to be tidied, and paperwork to sort out.

Accept that you will probably spend a good part of each half term break marking or report writing or preparing, but also understand that there are teachers who do jump on that plane straight after the final bell and return a week later looking bronzed and relaxed, ready to face anything that's thrown at them (sometimes literally). They may have to work a bit harder after school for a week or so to make up for not spending the week in despair, but the balance between work and life outside of work means that taking full advantage of the holiday gives these teachers the energy and enthusiasm to tackle the new term with gusto. Otherwise, you return to school wondering where the week has gone and feeling like there has been no holiday at all; instead, you have just gone through some kind of purgatory before reaching the gates of hell – sorry, school – once more.

This is especially true for the summer break. The last week of the school year is usually a time to wind down anyway, so while the pupils are watching the 'educational' video you are showing as a treat, use the time to file your worksheets or pack away books. When the pupils race out of the building with the taste of freedom within reach, you should do the same too. At least, give it a try. I don't know how much evidence there is in the rumour that many teachers simply fade away after retiring because they are not used to unwinding, but better to hedge your bets and look at your summer break as a practice for a long and stress-free retirement.

The last boy scout

My own experience of school was not always a happy one. Although I started secondary school bright-eyed and bushy-tailed, by the time I'd been through the mill of teenage hormones I was definitely not prefect material. Strangely, it seemed like most of my fellow classmates clamoured to be prefects or run the tuck shop or edit the school magazine, and I was gratified that my hunch about their ulterior motive was right: they just wanted good references on their university application forms. And possibly also the power to make younger pupils cower in terror for running down the corridors.

I believed that working to rule was a good principle. I was not quite sure what it meant exactly, but I knew there was no way an employer was going to get free labour out of me to fill their own pockets. With that attitude, imagine my surprise upon entering the school environment once more, only to find all those prefects had grown up and turned into teachers.

Here they were, volunteering to sit on committees that discussed everything from new uniform ideas to spending the ICT budget. Then they were running clubs at lunchtime and after school for no kind of overtime pay. Then came the even bigger commitments: staff to accompany over-excited sweet-scoffing kids for 48 hours on a coach that was part of the short break to France, somebody needed to design and make the costumes for the school production, someone else needed to give up their weekend to drive the minibus so that the debating team could attend a competition. I shook my head in disbelief at times, finding it hard to comprehend why you would want to give up your precious free time to do something that seemed above and beyond the call of duty.

Can you guess what happened next? Slowly, I got sucked in. First of all it started with a theatre trip which wouldn't return to school until midnight, but meant that I missed an afternoon of lessons that included the rudest boy I had ever met. Fair swap, I thought. Then came the annual residential that was organized by my department, and for which they really needed me to go, almost to the point of begging and bribery. It was exhausting. It was non-stop worry and head-counting and checking details and organizing children who could barely dress themselves and got homesick, but we had a great time. By the following weekend I almost forgot I hadn't had a day off for twelve days, and that four of those days had consisted of only five hours off duty (for sleeping!).

Pouncing on a willing residential trip goer, other teachers saw me as a pawn to be exchanged among departments, and I got to see new parts of the country, as well as many a motorway service station. I started to

develop a new skill of not retching violently whenever a
child was sick near me on the bus, and my supermarket
loyalty card began to show the data miners a warped
picture of myself, as I racked up the points for hundreds
of pounds of oven chips, bread rolls and bottles of squash.

But that wasn't all. I started two lunchtime clubs and
got so carried away that I organized competitive leagues
with neighbouring schools just for the satisfaction of
watching our school see off the toffs from up the road.
Having strong opinions about the way in which the
school was being run, it was all I could do to stop myself
becoming a nuisance and joining the school improvement
committee. What had happened to me? I was turning
into the last boy scout, into that cliché of a teacher at
whom I had scoffed only a short while ago.

However, I do have my limits. While I don't mind
volunteering for extra-curricular activities, and enjoy
working with the children outside of lesson time, I do
retain my right to say no. Unfortunately, that's not
always the way that everyone else sees it, especially the
management team. There are certain expectations placed
upon you as a teacher that you are not always willing or
able to fulfil. Sometimes it's as simple as the choice
between getting coursework marked on time and attending the school fete, or between finishing the reports for
the deadline and helping with after school play rehearsals.
That's without confessing to have an outside life with its
own obligations and appointments. I may well be glow-
ered at in the morning meeting when the staff are
thanked for supporting the Christmas fete, but I know
what would really hit the fan had I not finished writing
my form group's reports.

Top tips

Contributing to the extra-curricular activities in your school will be expected. If your spare time for this type of thing is limited, find out which events are the most high profile, where your face really should be seen, and which you can avoid. If you don't want to be at the beck and call of your colleagues when they need a helping hand with their particular project, start up your own activity. This could be a lunchtime club that meets for half an hour each week, either based on the subject you teach, or on your own particular interests.

For extra brownie points enter a select group of pupils into a national competition, whether it's story writing or technology projects. This way, not only are you credited with raising the profile of the school, but you also stand the chance of a few days out of school attending regional finals if you all put in the effort.

It is easy to be taken for granted and if you give away your favours too freely, you will find yourself put upon. Although it's great to spend time with the children outside of normal lessons, and you get to see sides of them that don't perhaps come across in your classes, stretching yourself across too many extra-curricular commitments is exhausting, and being forced to give up your precious spare time should not be part of the package.

Have a break before you have a breakdown

What exactly does breaktime mean, anyway? A break from the kids? A chance to tidy up the classroom before it all starts again? Not enough time to boil the kettle and drink your coffee? An opportunity to detain misbehaving pupils? Just enough time to get to the staff toilets, queue, and race back to the other end of the school where your classroom is? Playground duty?

It's no wonder teachers can feel stressed by the end of the day. Lunchtimes might consist of putting up displays (whatever the new workload agreement might advise), running clubs, attending rehearsals, phoning parents, raiding stock cupboards, photocopying, supervising detention, canteen duty, helping pupils who have been absent to catch up, marking, preparing, trying to find a printer that works to print out your worksheet for next lesson, chasing down the only set of textbooks you need for after lunch, or trying to find another member of staff you desperately need to talk to.

You might even have time to eat lunch. There are teachers who are stalwarts of the staffroom, who sink down into their favourite chairs each and every lunchtime; at least they always seem to be there when you pop your head round for five minutes. Maybe they are the same teachers who waste their valuable holiday time haunting the corridors of the school building, preparing or clearing up because they didn't want to relinquish their lunch breaks.

Top tips

There is something to be said for spending some of your lunchtime in the staffroom. It's a change of scene, and a change of conversation – this may well be your only chance all day to participate in conversation with adults. Or at least to listen to some outrageous gossip about the headteacher. The staffroom gives you an opportunity to discuss unruly pupils, and it can be a great comfort to discover that you're not the only one who struggles to contain a particular class. If things can seem out of perspective in the classroom, having a laugh about them with other members of staff can make you realize that it's not just you that Year 9 wind up.

Make sure that some of your breaktime resembles just that: a break from the constant rushing around. At least until one of your form members knocks on the staffroom door asking for you because of some emergency of epic proportions, such as forgetting their dinner money or getting a splinter.

Sometimes, though, the staffroom may seem to you to be a stressful place in its own intimidating way. Maybe it's a hive of gossip that you just don't want a part of. Workplace bullying is a topic that often comes up when teachers cite the specific stresses of their job. You might just dislike the company of the teachers who stake a claim to their corner of the staffroom. It could be that you don't see eye to eye with the teacher who regularly allows members of one of your teaching groups to wander the school on errands when they should be catching up with their coursework with you, but don't feel qualified to question their authority.

In this case, show what an asset you are to the school by throwing yourself into extra-curricular activities. After all, a change can be as good as a rest. If I sit down for more than ten minutes at lunchtime I'm tempted to snooze, and it's very difficult to drag myself back up again and get enthused for a long afternoon. You don't have to make work for yourself; if you don't want to run your own club or society, find another colleague who already does something you could help out with.

Fresh air is a good stress buster, especially if you would

otherwise never see the light of day between parking your car first thing, and staggering out again in the evening. In this case, you could offer to help out with a sports practice or nature club, and ensure you get your daily dose of daylight. Invest in a warm waterproof, because winter is the time that most of us crave to see the daylight, especially if it's not yet light when you arrive at school in the morning, and almost dark again when you leave. There are many ways to maximize your own chances of well-being while combining them with school activities. You don't have to think you must conform to the stereotype of the teacher swilling coffee in the staff-room every breaktime.

Sports Day

There are certain occasions when horrific childhood memories come flooding back to you as a teacher. For some, it may be the smell of fear in the exam hall on a sunny May morning. For me, it's Sports Day.

Now, I'm not completely unsporty. I exercise regularly, and even enjoy it. But I have never seen the point of Sports Day. It's just a big exercise in showing off, as the same kids triumph in track and field, whilst the others shiver in their shorts and are forced to throw small yet wrist-bendingly heavy balls, or whack their ankles on hurdles, or trot around the track whilst under the scrutiny of the entire school.

Teachers either take immediate control of their chosen activity or wait to be allocated a role, depending on whether the PE teacher picks you for their team or not. After picking up the high jump pole for the five hundred and twelfth time with a fixed grin of encouragement plastered across your face as your back clicks once again, crowd control looks like a cushy job. This is until you arrange a swap and realize that the kids are not going to sit in lines, pick up their sweet wrappers, or stop booing, however much you try to make yourself heard.

Top tips

My tips for surviving Sports Day are as follows. Learn how to use the digital camera, and quickly make yourself indispensable as the official photographer. This is also a great excuse to disappear for a while every hour, to 'download the pictures'.

However, if another teacher beats you to this ploy, the symptoms of hayfever can be easy to feign with the help of a well-concealed onion. Even better is the sprained ankle approach, which should afford you a seat in the sun far away from errant javelins. Or, if your school is desperate for helpers, you will be given a stopwatch and be made a finishing line judge, which is virtually Sports Day royalty.

In the exam hall

Exam time is an abiding memory for many people of their own school days, maybe because it was the last time they were obliged to enter a school building, or because whenever spring begins to change into a warm and pleasant summer, it reminds them of being trapped in a stuffy and uncomfortable hall, staring down at a list of questions with mild panic.

These days, exam time is almost a national symbol of

falling standards: an excuse by the press to ridicule easy questions and expose the latest 'questions for sale' scam, as well as showing up the incompetency of exam boards who set the wrong questions.

But now exams are not just consigned to hayfever season. With modular AS levels, GNVQs, SATs and the good old GCSEs, exam season is rather extended, meaning more disruption to teaching timetables and room changes in schools everywhere. However, there's still a period of May and June where the exams are concentrated, and schools seize the opportunity to set internal exams too.

All of which brings me onto the horror of the exam hall. It may seem bad enough when you're the pupil, having given up valuable socializing time to revise, only to find your mind goes blank as you slide into your seat and rickety old desk, but at least there's something to think about for the next couple of hours. Invigilating in external exams just pips to the post the mind-numbing boredom of after school staff meetings, although both share the same tendencies towards drooping eyelids and clenched fists of frustration.

External exams require that the invigilators are just that – vigilant. Some wise guy thought the best way to do this was to refuse the invigilator any external stimulus, such as a book, and require that they spend the hour or so scanning the horizon of desks for pupils squinting at their neighbour's paper, or texting an online database for help, or unfurling strips of paper from their pencil cases. What this wise guy failed to realize was that staring into the distance in a warm sports hall, with the scent of freshly cut grass almost disguising the smell of sweating teenagers and minty chewing gum, induces a kind of trance, where it is actually possible to sleep with your eyes open. I'm sure there are gurus on spiritual retreats in far-flung places who have strived for years to attain this kind of meditation, so I'm now pleased to reveal this short cut: an hour's worth of invigilation duty and you too can achieve this strange state of semi-consciousness.

I believe that this is the reason teachers take to pacing the aisles between desks with such fervour, peering at exam papers and the dandruff flaking on anxious scalps. It's not primarily to look for pupils cheating. It is, in fact, the only way to prevent a total body shutdown. There are also reports of games that teachers can play during invigilation periods, a few of which I will summarize here. Each game can be played by two teachers.

The first can be called 'Good kid or bad kid?'. Player one stands by one of the pupils that they teach, and player two has to guess whether that child is good or bad, indicating their answer by using a pre-determined sign. If player two is correct, player one steps to the side of the hall and player two can move in to have their turn. The first player with ten correct guesses in a row is the winner, and the loser has to make their breaktime beverage.

The second game can be seen in action on Channel 4's series *Teachers*. It involves giving out the most paper in the exam hall. Both players start off with equally sized piles, and the first one to get rid of their pile is the winner. There is inevitably cheating in this game, by giving out paper even to pupils who don't need it, but if one player catches their opponent doing this, the cheater has forfeited the game.

A third suggestion for a game requires a little preparation in advance. Palm-sized pieces of paper bearing legends such as 'most piercings', 'ugliest', 'thickest glasses', 'smelliest', 'most hair gel', 'most eye-liner' and so on can be taken into the exam hall. The two players take it in turns to select a card from the top of the pile, then have two minutes to locate and stand by the pupil that best fits the description. A kinder variation could be to have a list of animals, with teachers seeking out pupils who most resemble a duck or a snake.

While these games may well come in for criticism, they do allow the teachers to remain mentally alert, and to cover great areas of the exam hall with efficiency.

Top tips

To play invigilation games, you do need a willing partner. Unfortunately, you will probably find yourself scheduled to work alongside some grumpy old git of a teacher who actually enjoys the time where his only responsibility is dashing around the hall with an inflated sense of self-worth, and flicking through the exam questions with a frown on his face as he realizes that he no longer knows enough to gain a GCSE in any subject outside of his own.

If you have nobody to play with, look on the bright side: you are in the sports hall and so you could utilize the time wisely to improve your fitness. Don't be tempted by the monkey bars, however; you could make the most of the pacing time by investing in a pedometer, which measures how many steps you take. During each session, try to outpace yourself from the previous session. Not only have you then completed your recommended exercise quota for the day, but your calves will feel firmer, especially if you pause by a desk every now and again to peer at a paper, and employ the motion of rocking backwards and forwards between your two feet. Bending down to recover fallen pens and protractors is beneficial for your waist or thighs, depending on your action, and holding paper aloft for at least three minutes every half an hour will strengthen your arm muscles.

A great exercise for your bottom and thighs will become a natural part of your regime: every time you go to sit down, one of the pupils will inevitably raise their hand, meaning you pause just an inch above the chair before having to stand up again. Try this a few times and you'll feel gratitude towards every child that asks a dumb question.

If the physical workout doesn't appeal, force yourself to give your mind a workout. For every pupil in the exam hall whose name you know, think of three adjectives to describe them that begin with the same letter as the first letter of their name. Sure, it's immature, but to the outside world you will appear alert and vigilant, which is preferable to sliding off your seat sideways in a torpor.

Marking madness

It's been bothering me that I'm one of the laziest teachers I know. It's not something I've wanted to own up to, but I feel it's time for a confessional tone.

It's not that I'm lazy in the classroom. I'm certainly not the type of teacher who sits at their desk during a lesson, letting the little scamps get on with it. How else would they feel threatened into working if I wasn't towering over them, sneaking around in non-squeaky shoes, and sweeping down to pounce on note passing and the furtive unwrapping of chewing gum?

I'm not lazy in my preparation either. I love making resources: worksheets and handouts and games. I am master of the Clip-art and the Internet image search, hunting down the perfect illustration for each topic's worksheet with only a small degree of obsession, even though I know my lovingly created resources will be graffitied upon, torn, screwed up, and destined for recycling before the hour is out.

To my colleagues, I am efficient. It's me they ask about the time and place of meetings, knowing I write them in my planner with anally retentive precision. They admire my filing system, improvised with cardboard boxes bearing the legends of past usage: *Tomatoes* and *Apples*. Reports written on time? No problem. Forms filled in by the deadlines? A day before, my friend. Instant recall ability of each lesson's relevance to the National Curriculum? Yep indeedy, with the confidence of the professional bluffer, of course.

But it has started to strike me that as I run up the stairs each morning, and straight back down again each afternoon, that I am unburdened by the boxes and bags of exercise books that other teachers lug about. This was underlined by a recent conversation with a colleague, where we grumbled about our early starts, share of the housework, lost Sunday afternoons, and so on, compared to the easy and unburdened lives of our respective non-teaching partners.

It suddenly hit me that my colleague was talking about marking books every night of the week, whereas I was referring to the fact that my pottery class clashed with my daily dose of TV drama. I didn't admit it of course, but carried on letting my colleague think that I too was referring to book marking, while hoping that my thoughts didn't leak out of my brain and start rearranging themselves in picture form around the top of my head.

Following further investigations, I've discovered that another colleague's breakdown and subsequent revision of contract to part-time status was brought on by reducing the number of free weekday evenings by one to zero, in order to keep on top of coursework marking. Yet another colleague takes full advantage of insomnia to mark books well into the wee small hours.

All of which makes me feel incredibly lazy. By the time I get home I've already had at least a twelve hour day, so I'm usually extremely reluctant to do another six hours of work-related stuff. I don't mind hunting down resources or making a worksheet or two, but the thought of rising out of my armchair during peak viewing time to start trying to decipher some of the rubbish that passes for classwork makes my stomach lurch. I've been there, done that, and almost had the breakdown. Besides, how else am I going to 'keep it real' with 'da kids' if I can't communicate with them on the simplest level about what's going on in the charts and on The Street? (I'm referring to *Coronation Street* here, I'd rather not think about what goes on out on real streets after dark.) Isn't it my duty to make the kids feel included and relevant?

So yes, I feel lazy compared to the slavish dedication of some of my colleagues. But I don't feel guilty now that I've thought it through. The books get marked, eventually. It's just a case of varying activities in the classroom so that not every lesson ends up with written work. And I feel like a more efficient teacher for my evenings of leisurely pursuits, like pottery and football and operatics. Okay, I'll admit it, we all know I'm talking about watching TV, don't we?

Top tips

If marking is getting on top of you, there are several things you can do to ease the burden. Not every task you set has to result in a written activity, whatever your subject is. You just have to be creative, and your pupils will enjoy the variety that your lessons offer. From group role-plays to individual presentations, having them concentrate on an oral activity means you can mark them as they make their presentation. You can also involve the rest of the class as an audience. Give them something to do as they listen, such as thinking of at least one question to ask the speaker, or allocating marks to each group based on the criteria you give them.

Similarly, homework doesn't have to result in a written task. You could ask pupils to research or prepare something to bring in for the lesson next week. They could learn spellings for a test, or work on ongoing project work. To prevent them thinking this is homework they can wriggle out of because you won't be marking it, make sure you test them or ask to see their research on the deadline.

Peer marking is a useful activity, especially if your subject encourages the drafting and redrafting of work. Ask pairs of pupils to swap work and look out for incorrect spellings, missing punctuation, and so on, which they can circle with a pencil. Ask them to think of three things their partner could add to their work, or three things they could improve. Hopefully, this kind of exercise will teach children to check their own work before handing it in, and they will also learn the techniques of careful proofreading.

Another method for reducing the agony that marking can be is to tell the class what in particular you will be marking for in a certain piece of work. This could be anything from paragraphing to how well they have answered the question, but it means that you don't have to get side-tracked by correcting spellings and presentation for every single piece of work.

Group project work can give you a breather from marking a particular class's work for a while, and is especially useful if you are trying to balance your marking schedule with your other classes, who have just submitted large pieces of coursework. The project work can last several lessons without you having to mark anything, especially if you instruct each group to have one member responsible for proofreading. If the groups produce something like a wall display, stick the finished projects up around the room, and let the groups circulate and mark each others' work based on criteria you give them. This type of exercise is beneficial not just for you: it enables the pupils to see how they could improve their own work next time, and to draw conclusions as to what makes a successful project.

With marking, teachers very often find they reap what they sow. You may well decide you want a quiet lesson with the pupils working hard on individual written work, but you will have to mark what they have produced. If you vary your learning activities you will have to become an intrinsic and active part of each lesson, instead of having half an hour to sit at your desk, desperately trying to mark books for the next lesson. But this also means that you won't have to spend as much of your free time ploughing through a dog-eared pile of work.

Surviving a hangover

When I was on teaching practice, a sage piece of advice was handed down to me by a harassed member of my department: after the first time, you will never attempt teaching with a hangover again. But did I listen? Indeed, in those hazy days of teaching just two or three lessons a day, interspersed with easy access to the never ending supply of cold Kit-Kats from the vending machine, a hangover was an unwelcome yet inevitable part of the routine. The banging, the shouting, the screaming ... was that me, the kids, or the voices in my head? The nausea and dizziness was not helped by the enforced standing up (or swaying, as it seemed).

But the vicious circle of life means that a bad day at school these days is followed by a couple of beers, some wine, perhaps a chug or two of whisky ... it always seems like a good idea at the time. At least it cheers up my spirit in the evening, but come the morning it's a very different tale. And the sad part about getting older is that even a solitary glass of wine with dinner is enough to induce a headache some mornings.

If the hair dryer sounds too loud in the morning, then I know I'm in for a rough ride. Hungover teaching usually goes one of two ways. The first way is preferable, as the day shimmies past like an alternate reality. To minimize the noise damage and save a ravaged throat, lots of activities can be knocked together that require almost independent work from the kids. The favourite is aptly called 'making a poster', which requires only coloured paper and a faint glimmer of an idea. Very limited educational content, in my opinion, but if pushed I could justify the lesson to anyone who cared or dared to ask – from curriculum specific content to key skills to citizenship (that means things like sharing glue and working together without a punch-up). The kids love it, aside from the occasional squabble or slap over the stationery, and so noise levels are peacefully low.

Ah yes, making a poster. Make a poster to show what a certain character was like or how a combustion engine works. Make a poster explaining why beggars would be hanged in a Tudor village or showing the rules of multiplication. Make a poster of whatever you like because I can't be bothered arguing; just look busy. That's one of the most important lessons you need for life anyway.

The first hangover solution requires a minimal five minutes of shouting at the beginning of the lesson, probably followed by ten minutes of repetition to the usual idiots who weren't listening, before the luxury of sitting down at the desk with thumping head in hands.

The responsibly hungover teacher will also take a dizzy stagger around the room from time to time, ostensibly to check on progress, in reality to make sure nobody at the back is texting on their mobile phone, and also to stay awake of course. There's also the delicate matter of wind, but good timing of the classroom wander means there are a plethora of small victims to blame.

This is also one of the times when those 'magic moments' of teaching take place. In a relaxed hungover state of blurry reality, the pressures of making sure that every child has negotiated the clearly defined learning objectives of the lesson go out the window, and allows the teacher to have a good laugh at their crappy attempts at drawing and writing, thanking the lord that they were never such a slow-wit. I guarantee, pass a classroom where a teacher is honestly laughing – and I don't mean in a manic or sarcastic way – and that teacher is probably enjoying the detached reality of a hangover. Double guaranteed if the kids are making posters.

The second type of hangover, though, is not the fun and games of the first. It is cruel, vicious, and probably some kind of karmic payback. It's usually raining and the room gets stuffy, with the steamed up windows only adding to the oppressive and claustrophobic atmosphere.

The kids are shouting, argumentative and uncooperative – not much change there, I know – but the noise is intensified when it rattles around in my vacuous skull while my booze-shrivelled brain cowers in the corner.

To make matters worse, the need to shout frequently arises, and the booze's laxative effect starts to be quite a pressing matter – fine for office workers who can saunter to the toilet at will, but not for the classbound teacher who can't desert their post for another two hours. It's a miserable situation, and one that, knowing the spite of Sod's Law, will probably be topped by a surprise lesson observation or the headteacher dropping in to discuss something you suddenly remember should have been prepared last night when you decided to push the books out of the way and start knocking back the beers.

At least you know that, like all things, this time will pass. Albeit slowly and excruciatingly. And perhaps with some new insight into the laughable stupidity of some of your pupils. And of course, the stupidity of yourself, for drinking on a school night when you should know better.

Top tips

Well there's the obvious point here: don't drink on a school night. But that's not my tip at all, because while I may veer between pessimism and optimism, I know for sure that I'm a realist too.

There's a serious point to be made here too. Sometimes, you may struggle into work feeling genuinely ill. Your head may be banging, you may be starting to get a cold, or your tummy feels slightly dodgy, and you really don't know how you're going to get through the day.

Make sure you have a back up plan. One sunny

September day, at the beginning of the school year when you know what classes you've got but you still haven't taken any books in to mark, spend an hour or so preparing your 'first aid' lessons. These should be a ready-made lesson, at least one for each group you teach, that can be used as a stand-alone lesson requiring minimal fuss and individual quiet work.

Stash them away in your filing cabinet just in case you come in one day feeling wobbly and incapable, and your weak and perhaps hungover self will look back on bright and breezy self with an immense amount of gratitude.

6 Money's too tight to mention

Money mismanagement

Very occasionally, the urge to do your job of teacher well
will overtake common sense and past experience. A long-
buried spark of enthusiasm will be fired up, and you find
yourself trotting to your line manager with your great
idea for a new initiative to combat underachieving,
racism or bullying. The only thing is, your idea needs
resources, and that means finding some money in some
budget somewhere, which is where your idea ends,
doomed never to become reality.

Funding will always be a sensitive issue for schools.
Teacher numbers decrease if the powers that be demand
the money that a school is allocated should be deployed
elsewhere, for example in relieving teaching staff of
administrative duties. But then there are other funds and
accounts that the school does have complete control over,
and which are decided upon by budgetary committees.
These committees will usually be made up of senior
teachers and governors. As they sit there dishing up the
spoils between departments who won't be able to buy
any new text books next year, they munch their way

through silver trays of triangular sandwiches and fancy cream cakes. We teachers know this happens because the next morning in the staffroom we are shown the remains of the curly-cornered sandwiches and told we may feast on these treats at breaktime. What kind of budgetary planning allows each committee to spend the cost of four text books on fancy and unnecessary sandwiches every time they meet?

Top tips

Some teachers don't mind paying for school things out of their own pockets. For some it may be an addiction to buying books that would enhance teaching of certain topics. This seems perfectly normal, because most of us love books anyway, and know deep down that they give us far more pleasure than the children feel when they pore over the grainy photocopies that we distribute. Other teachers go further, but if you are unwilling to squander your hard-earned wages when you see the wastage elsewhere, then try some creative accounting.

Next time the plate of sandwiches and petit fours is left wilting in the staffroom, make the most of the opportunity. If they are still palatable, you've got your lunch sorted, and the pound that you would have spent in the canteen on equally soggy chips and cheese can go towards buying some new colouring pencils or something else cheap and useful. Pound shops and supermarkets often sell very cheap stationery.

If the sandwiches look too far gone to be edible, they can still be useful. Take them as a prop for your next lesson: a still life in art, perhaps, or the basis of a role-play with your drama group. On the subject of props, if the food was served on shiny silver platters and you're sure the catering company won't demand their return, you have some flexible resources at your fingertips: shiny shields for your knights to hold while demonstrating the mediaeval feudal system? A three dimensional element for your wall display on the solar system? Be creative! After all, these trays of sandwiches were probably the reason your department couldn't afford any backing paper for wall displays in the first place.

They could be conversation starters in languages lessons, perhaps for role-plays in cafeteria situations or for extending food and shopping vocabulary. Go on, teach the children to complain about stale sandwiches in three different languages!

Depending on the state of the sandwiches, they could be useful for bacteria analysis in science, or lessons on hygiene and presentation in food technology. Think laterally, too. After all, if you were teaching in a developing country where you had no text books or photocopier you would frequently have to make the best of what you did have. Take this survivalist approach, and suddenly that wilting tray of sandwiches becomes a prompt for creative writing, a small business set-up idea in business studies, and budgeting or portion control in maths. Your maths group may even come up with some solutions for the school budgetary committee.

Day-tripping – or lack of it

Teachers are often sent glossy brochures from companies or attractions telling them how great it would be for their school to visit. Theme parks apparently make great places to study design and technology, physics, maths, and no doubt the art of how to queue. Then there are castles, zoos, battlefields, theatres, nature reserves, museums, exhibitions, outdoor centres, and so on. What better way to enrich the curriculum! After all, a day out and change of scene can be far more memorable than a day staring out of a steamy classroom window. Even for the kids.

But if a trip is an essential part of the curriculum, then parents are not legally obliged to pay. Most do, of course, but then there are some that really can't afford it, and the money has to be found from somewhere ... it's a lot of hassle, and it could all be avoided if the trip never took place at all. And have I even mentioned the cost of supply cover for the teachers accompanying the trip? We can't just take parents any more, not without paying and waiting for their security clearance. That, unfortunately, is why all those glossy brochures get left in pigeon-holes in the staffroom.

Instead the teacher stands there in front of the class, trying to bring to life Act III of *Romeo and Juliet*, something which the theatre down the road is doing so much more professionally and memorably.

Top tips

See what's available in the local vicinity, preferably in walking distance. For example, graveyards can bring alive (if you'll excuse the wording) the ideas in gothic literature. Even a sunny day can feel chillier if you take your reading of *Frankenstein* or *Dracula* out among the tombstones. Graveyards are an example of local history, whether that means showing attitudes to religion over time or attempting to create family trees, or even surveying the life expectancies during certain periods.

Naturally, graveyards can prompt debate in religious studies, and are a useful exercise in mental arithmetic. They should bring out the artist in even the moodiest teenager, and often provide a refuge for wildlife. Just make sure it's the right type of wildlife beforehand – maybe bribe the local winos to take their super strength lager elsewhere for the day.

Make the most of people prepared to come into the school rather than you taking the children there. Local museums often have artefact collections for loan, and many museum collections are now online. These can be useful for history of course, but also art, English, languages, and so on. For example, IT students could set up databases of information, using online museum collections as examples. Or they could design leaflets for visitors to an exhibition of their own choosing, selecting several objects from the museum website to include in their personalized exhibition. Geographers and science students could discover more about rocks and volcanoes by tapping into a geology collection. Many are just as accessible online as they are behind a glass case in a museum.

Theatre companies can come to perform in school, and there are a number of initiatives like the 'recycling road-show' who can visit, usually bringing with them prepared worksheets and activities which will fulfil national curriculum criteria. Studying the Civil War? Get in touch with the local re-enactment group who could send in a fully costumed cavalier or roundhead, who will hopefully have a studious knowledge on the workings of the flint-lock pistol beyond the textbook's dry list of battles and dates.

It's much easier to take over the school hall for the afternoon than to organize trusted parent helpers, coaches, packed lunches and dwindling budgets. And knowing that the children won't get lost or injure themselves in a freaky worst-case scenario from your carefully prepared risk assessment should help you as the teacher to enjoy the experience too.

Extra-curricular spending

Now, for once, this is not a grumble about teacher wages. Depending on where you are in the country, they can go a long way, and unfortunately they sometimes have to!

This is about what teaching wages get spent on. Let's start with red pens to mark books and black pens to write reports and mark the register. Pens may be cheap, but they're used up at a frightening rate. It's a good job that ink isn't an endangered resource. The danger comes from lending your pen to a colleague, or leaving it on your desk for a moment, or lending it to a forgetful child. The pen is then whisked into another dimension, never to be seen again. Or chewed to pieces by that grubby little tyke that never has his or her own equipment because of their tendency to reduce the toughest of biros into a splintered plastic mess.

But hey, pens – I had to provide my own when I worked on the tills at a top supermarket as a Saturday cashier. Borrow a pen from any supermarket cashier to sign your cheque and you'll get some insight into their personality: the last one I borrowed was a souvenir from Butlins, and others inform me of which bank their wages get paid into.

So what expenditure is unique, yet necessary, to teaching? Buying colouring pencils, pens, glues, staples and other stationery sundries that the school passed over buying in order to purchase text books, of all things. Taking home and washing at your own expense tea-towels, lab coats, protective aprons and other specialist paraphernalia that are used and abused by the kids. Buying your own document wallets and plastic pockets to file school resources. And finally – the cheaper version of therapy for stressed out teachers – the bottle of gin/wine/scotch for the two hours on Friday evening between getting home and falling asleep.

Top tips

Make good friends with your local businesses or any offices in the area. Very often offices will throw out huge numbers of document wallets and folders because they have already been written on, but these are perfectly usable otherwise. If you have no contacts with the businesses, some of your pupils will have parents or neighbours with these connections. Or go straight to the source. Use tutorial time or English lessons to put letter writing skills to good use, and practise writing formal letters to companies asking them to remember your school or department when they spring clean their stock cupboards.

There are teachers who have already jumped on the entrepreneurial bandwagon. They buy very cheap stationery in bulk, for example 25 pencils for a pound, and then sell the pencils to children who haven't brought their own, usually at about 10p each. Any profit made over a term is then used to buy something that benefits the whole class, such as colouring pencils that can be borrowed during lessons, or prizes for the hardest working groups.

Prizes and presents are another area that can add up. Rightly or wrongly, there is a trend for teachers to run end of term or end of teaching unit quizzes, and woe betide the teacher who can only offer a gold star to the winners. I'm not advocating dishing out high fat and high sugar treats to the increasingly obese, allergic and hyperactive generation, but if you were given far too many boxes of chocolates at Christmas, end of term is the ideal time to redistribute your bounty, sparingly.

Or once again, gel pens and patterned pencils amuse most children and also ensure that everybody in your class has at least something with which to write, and can be bought out of any pencil selling profits you have accumulated during the year. Keep your eyes peeled at any conferences or trade shows you attend, which are often great sources of pens, yo-yos, keyrings or other small plastic novelties that will suffice for prizes.

Alternatively, rise to the giddy heights of Head of Department where you will have control over some part of the budget, and can lavish a steady stream of red pens upon your grateful staff.

7 Dealing with colleagues

Gossip

There are so many things to remember when you start a new job, but there's one invaluable lesson to be upheld if your job involves going anywhere near a staffroom. It's nothing to do with those old chestnuts of sitting in the wrong chair or using somebody else's coffee cup, milk or fridge space. The lesson that will stand you in good stead is to NEVER say anything to anybody beyond small talk about the weather until you know who hates who, who tells what to who else, who once pissed off somebody else six years ago and has never been forgiven, and so on. In other words, who's bitching for which team.

In fact, discussing the weather can be a useful test of where conversation trickles when your back is turned. You'll know how far your comments go when a kid comes up to tell you that, 'Mrs X said you're always moaning about the weather'. All you have to do then is work out how Mrs X knows when you only told Mr A.

It all seems so innocent when you first start. There are so many names to learn that it really is best to say nothing of any significance about anyone else to anybody at all. Otherwise, it will be an awful stomach-dropping moment when you realize that Miss Mills is actually the mother of that wretch in your Year 9 group, and that she is married to Mr Smythe, who is not related to Mrs Smythe, despite what you saw going on in the science lab on your way to moan about the Year 9 wretch to the head of year, who happens to be Miss Mills' best friend since teacher training college.

Confusing? Oh yes. Particularly if you fall victim of any of the following:

- only knowing the first names of some teachers and the surnames of others, and not being able to match up either of these with the sets of initials by which they are known on the edge of the pigeonholes or in the staff handbook;
- assuming that teachers who drink tea together like each other;
- assuming that teachers who stay huddled in their department's office can bear the sight of each other;
- underestimating the length and breadth of the headteacher's network of gossip, which can seem to permeate every social network within the school;
- believing that an after school drink will endear you to your colleagues, instead of stigmatizing you as you choose to socialize with 'that lot', as 'that lot' try to fill your mind with the misdemeanours of absent colleagues.

Even when you've been in the school for a couple of years there can be surprises. And they are usually nasty, in the way that exposing yourself as a gossip when you only said one thing to the wrong person once will do. These days I like to think of myself as a sponge, soaking up the remains of the spilt guts that cross my path, but

never squeezing them out in public. I do slip up occasionally though, and it's a horrible feeling. You know you're
heading down that stony path when you catch yourself
saying something to a colleague that starts with, 'Well, I
heard ...' or 'Apparently ...'. This kind of thing makes
me feel about 14 years of age all over again, but maybe
working in a school brings you out in a rash of gossip; a
result of being in close contact with teenage hormones
for too long.

And perhaps there is a reason for all this juvenile behaviour. Ten minute chats about the weather at breaktime
aside, contact with colleagues in a school is fleeting. Most
of the working day is spent in the company of children,
and even if there are other adults in the classroom,
perhaps to support children with learning difficulties,
there's no time to chat and find out something about
their lives.

On the other hand, there are long-standing teachers in
my school who are extremely good friends. They car-
share, baby-sat for each other once upon a time, meet up
in pubs, have dinner at each others' houses, and even end
up marrying each other. Maybe it's just a slower process
in a school than elsewhere. Or maybe the gossip that
divides some of the staff binds others, so that the only
thing they have in common is a shared irrational hatred
of somebody else, usually middle or senior management.
At least, that's what I heard ...

Top tips

I can only reiterate what I stated above: find out about
the complex social relationships at work in your staffroom before wading in with your opinion. If you have
been in one teaching post for a long time, you forget that

once upon a time you knew nothing about the ancient grudges of failed internal promotions or clandestine affairs. When you move to a new post, however long you have been teaching, you have to start all over again, being the newest part of the complex social network that exists among the staff at any school. One remark out of place to the wrong person will be remembered for a long time, especially when you only meet up with these people during short tea breaks.

Being sporty

Sometimes it's hard to be a pupil, we're all aware of that. One of the worst trials is surely the test of picking the sports teams. It can be such a trauma for some children that it's almost a cliché: the skinny kids, the fat kids, the asthmatic kids, the shy kids, huddled together in their ill-fitting shorts and shirts, waiting to be chosen for a side by the lithe-of-limb and sporty-in-heart team captain.

By the time we're grown up such ordeals are, thankfully, only rarely encountered. That's not to say that even as teachers we never endure such trials. From the interview stages for jobs, when the existing team of teachers – and at times, pupils – decide which of the shivering and shaking applicants should join their team, to the triumph of being chosen to go on the all-expenses paid beano of the school ski trip or study exchange to somewhere exotic, the sports team picking process can prepare most children for the disappointments, struggles and successes of adult life.

This section, though, is about the endless gloating of PE teachers in staff meetings. Let me explain. Say you teach a subject other than PE. You work hard, you've got books to mark, steamy classrooms on wet days, smelly class-rooms on hot days, magic to perform with a broken stick of chalk and a scratched blackboard. Sometimes you might glance out of the window and see hoards of chil-dren pounding the running track, with one tracksuited figure loitering about with a stopwatch. Or, on your free lesson, you might pass the changing rooms and observe that even though lessons started 15 minutes ago, the PE lessons are still in the spraying deodorant and removing earrings stages.

Now I'm not saying that PE teachers have it easy. Having covered PE lessons before, I'm aware of how stressful it can be to deal with lost kit, forged notes, thefts from the changing rooms, smelly feet, shenanigans in the showers, and all the other hassles before the kids are even out on the playing fields. I would hardly deny them the pleasures of next to no marking (in comparison – I know some PE teachers have lots of GCSE and AS work to plough through) because when I'm making the most of my lunch hour by putting up wall displays, planning, marking, etc, I know that the PE teacher is stoically coaching the football or hockey team, or setting up hurdles, or taking over-excited youngsters to play against another school team.

But come on, let's be honest here. It's not the hardest job in the world, is it? Whatever recruitment crises the profession is currently undergoing, PE is hardly a short-age subject. Time and time again, courses to train as PE teachers are oversubscribed, and I'm sure I've read reports that potential PE candidates always have shiny qualifica-tions in a broad range of subjects and could have their pick of jobs, but choose to use their expertise to get kids fit.

Here is the crux of what really annoys me. It's staff

meeting time. Or school assembly. Whatever you've done in the past week, and whatever subject you teach, there have been some successes. Maybe one of your pupils completed their coursework at long last. Maybe one class finally understood something just as you were beginning to despair. Maybe a particular child managed not to shout out for the whole lesson. But hang on, what's that the headteacher is saying? Well done to the rugby team, even though they lost their third match in a row? Let's have the netball team up here on the stage for a round of applause for thrashing the school in special measures down the road? And you – you in the fifth row – why aren't you applauding loudly?

Yep, this is what really gets my goat. Although I am actually a firm believer in phrases like 'a healthy mind in a healthy body', I hate feeling like a traitor to the 'school team' for not giving a stuff that our rounders team played in some semi-final somewhere. I certainly don't waste time laying awake at night wondering how the gym team did in the local competition. Why should I applaud like a deranged sea lion when the oafs in the football team, who constantly miss my lessons for matches or training, score a few more goals than the other team? And woe betide the next PE teacher who announces in our staff meeting that their team won this or that, and then looks round the gathered staff for their praise and admiration. I'm not even interested! Although I could demonstrate my own physical dexterity with a deft punch to their gloating chops.

Top tips

The issue that arises here is that anything which gives the school instant prestige is going to have priority over the run-of-the-mill actual teaching and learning that goes on every day. This can make life difficult if the Under 16 county javelin thrower is in your GCSE set, and has yet to produce a piece of coursework because he is too busy annihilating the competitors from neighbouring schools, in what is essentially a hunter–gatherer skill of not much use in the world of work (unless he plans to be a big game hunter or something).

Often the frustration on the teacher's side comes from only finding out that half the class is leaving for a hockey match once the lesson has started. It is extremely annoying to have planned to introduce a new and tricky topic, prepared the work and drawn up the diagrams on the board, only to discover that most of the boys have to leave in ten minutes to go and roll around in the mud.

Find out at the beginning of the school year if any of your pupils are in sports teams. Fixtures are usually drawn up well in advance, so ask either the pupils concerned, or better still the PE department, for a list of match dates. This can be amusing in itself, watching the PE teacher try to grapple with paperwork.

If you know that several members of your class will be absent, it will help you to plan something that they won't struggle to catch up with on their return. With the sporty type of child, it's far too optimistic to believe they will catch up with the missed work in their own time, because they will probably be too busy with lunchtime or after school practices.

You may have to grin and bear the bragging of the PE department, but you can minimize the disruption to your own lessons with a little foresight, and by efficient communication with your colleagues.

When your classroom is used and abused

Unfortunately, there comes a moment of realization when you're a teacher that not everybody is as competent as you. If you are a generally incompetent person anyway, you may be shocked to find out that this still applies.

For those of us lucky enough to have our own classroom, and not destined to haul around books and equipment between different floors or buildings, we can get quite possessive of our room. It might need several good coats of paint, it might be too hot when the sun beams through in the mornings, and maybe the desks constantly need propping up with wads of paper under a wonky leg, but a lot of time and effort goes into creating the best working environment possible. Wall displays are scrutinized regularly for missing drawing pins, desks are checked for new graffiti, and a small hoard of chalk or pens are kept handy from the latest raid on the stock cupboard.

So imagine the feeling of dismay when it seems that every time I return to my room after a lesson elsewhere, I seem to experience a hell dimension consisting of a floor carpeted with sweet wrappers, shelves adorned with bits of used tissue, wall displays hanging by one remaining drawing pin, and desks that tell playground tales of who is 4 who, and who else is a slag. I will spare you the more gruesome details of nasal contents.

I frequently glare at the departing teacher's back with scorn, incredulous at the sudden departure. Firstly, how dare they pretend to be so blind that they don't see the rubbish they are wading through to reach the door? Secondly, how dare they leave the rubbish for me to pick up, as I know that otherwise it's a clear message to my next class to help themselves to their sweets and then drop their rubbish too, or merely throw the existing rubbish around. Thirdly, what the hell went on in that lesson that could leave such a trail of destruction? Maybe the messy teacher has already had their punishment in the preceding hour, but as I dislodge those manky tissues yet again, it's hard to feel much sympathy.

Top tips

This can be a tricky subject to broach with your colleague. They have a responsibility to leave the room in a fit state for the next teacher, but if they are continually failing in this duty there are several things you can do.

Try to find out why they have allowed such a mess to be created. Were they called out of the room to take a phone call or deal with something else? Ask the kids. They will soon tell you how chaotic the teacher's lessons are, but remember to take what you hear with at least a slight pinch of salt. If the teacher is failing to control their classes, you could have a quiet word along the lines of how terrible 10B are, and then suggest some tactics that may have worked for you, whether you are basing your examples on that class or another. Or you could start with small requests: just ask them to keep an eye on the pupils sitting by the wall displays, saying that you are determined to track down the culprit who keeps pinching your drawing pins, and you have your suspects narrowed down to lessons on a Wednesday morning (or whenever it is). The last thing you want to do is tip over the edge somebody who is already on the verge of a nervous breakdown.

It could be that the teacher is just incompetent, or doesn't care, or is counting down the days to retirement and has given up trying to control the class. If they are leaving the school, the best thing to do is grit your teeth and count down the days with them. And then hope they don't come back to do supply work.

If the direct approach scares you, perhaps because this teacher is senior to you in the school hierarchy, there are some other tactics you could employ. Huge signs on the wall, by the bin, and by the door, ostensibly for the pupils, should remind colleagues to keep your room tidy. Change the positioning of the signs around every week so they are eye-catching. Make sure the bin is in an obvious place. If you know any of the pupils in that teaching group, ask them if they could make sure the room is tidy when they leave. This might result in no more than them blurting out at the end of their chaotic lesson that Mr/Ms so-and-so wants the room tidy, but it might stir the untidy teacher into action.

If there's no improvement, raise the issue at a staff meeting, even if it's just within your department. The senior member should then report back or write down in the minutes what your request is. This doesn't have to be specific. Allow the issue to remain hanging rather than directing the blame at any member of staff. Say something like you've noticed that the kids are becoming messier, and maybe you suspect that some of them have been sneaking in at breaktimes, because the classrooms you teach in are becoming more untidy. Ask that a message be passed onto staff to ensure rooms are tidy at the end of lessons, and that children are not allowed in unsupervised.

Hopefully you will find that one of these ways will improve the situation. There's no point in bitching about the incompetency of your colleague to other staff members, because that won't resolve your problem, although it might make you feel better!

8 Dealing with parents

Parents' evening

Like the football season, parents' evening season seems to grow longer every year. Parents' evenings do vary from school to school. Some allow the children to be present along with their parents. There are of course advantages and disadvantages to this. If the child sits down with the parent, the teacher is expected to know the name of that child, I suppose, but there are always a few that slip through the net. If the child isn't there, at least the parents can tell you who it is you are supposed to be talking about. If you don't know the child's name, there's not usually much to say about them anyway, which makes for an excruciating five minutes.

Some schools have a system of appointments to see each teacher, whereas others opt directly for the free-for-all that any type of system tends to disintegrate into anyway. At some schools, the timing of the parents' evening will coincide with prime-time TV viewing, which does affect the type of parents that turn up. Others are run for a few hours directly after school, meaning that commuting parents never receive any face-to-face feedback, but instead the school hall is filled with parents dragging around the broods of children they've just gathered from creche or neighbouring schools.

Parents' evenings are great from an anthropological point of view though. All those people in one claustrophobic school hall, suppressing their own school day memories and trying to look like they understand what they are being told. That's the teachers and parents alike! Like them or loathe them, the parents' evening can become an easier process once you know what to expect.

Top tips

You can ease the burden of parents' evening in advance. For weeks before, inform various children who slightly or grossly misbehave that you can't wait to see their parents. Perhaps even pocket some of the more daring notes they pass around class and tell them that their parents would love to see the work they produce in lessons. Come the evening itself, watch smugly as your charges guide their parents away from your table, then nip home early.

However, for the more determined parent, you should know what you're dealing with. Here are some of the more common categories of parents.

Aggressive parents

You usually know what to expect from the parents because you have, after all, got to know the child. It's at the moment when the burly red-faced father sits down that you realize that the child's cries of 'I'm going to get my dad up here' because you dared to hand out a detention were no idle threat at all. Aggressive parents refuse to accept that anything, from low exam marks and incomplete homework to the CCTV footage of the canteen being trashed, is their child's fault.

Sometimes this aggression can be well hidden at first. This is the most dangerous situation, as you can be lulled into a false sense of security. After showing their child's exercise book and reeling off some targets, you may well feel that these parents could help you and support your efforts in school by ensuring their little treasure does not bring in her mobile phone/gameboy/pet rat again. This is when the aggression bubbles to the surface and splatters you all over the face.

Aggressive parents are not class-specific. There is some overlap between this category and Well-informed parents, as well as my next category . . .

Trailer trash parents

I'm sorry to have to even mention this category at all. They don't all live in trailers of course, but if you imagine the stereotypical *Jerry Springer Show* brawling dimwits, you'll get some idea of this group of parents. It's the best reminder to stop the doziest kids snogging in the corner of the library at lunchtimes, because here you have a portent of things to come.

Trailer trash parents are usually just mother, and occasionally just father. I award a ten point bonus if a trailer trash couple attend together. Mother will turn up bedecked in her finest white tracksuit, hair scraped back into a greasy ponytail, and will spend most of the appointment trying to extract her chubby baby's fingers from the large array of gold chains she is wearing. She may stop to yell after her toddlers who have run off to play with the other teachers' legs, or to take a call on her flashy little mobile. She'll be extremely irritated that it's no smoking, and instead chomp her way through a packet of chewing gum. Why she's actually there is a bit of a mystery, as she doesn't listen to a thing you say, and you're not even sure she would understand or care anyway. In some cases she may bring with her a sour-faced older woman who could well be her mother, so that they can gang up on you if you say anything 'out of order' about their beloved child.

Trailer trash father may well belong in the 'Aggressive parents' category. Or he may seize the opportunity to try his various charms on you to excuse his child's behaviour, flirting while skirting the issues at hand. You know he's really only here to trawl the masses of single mothers who are desperate to get home in time for 'Neighbours'.

Nervous parents

Ah, bless, probably my favourite parents. They're not sure how to act around teachers, and still feel like they should be on their best behaviour. They've dressed smartly for the occasion and they listen really carefully to everything that you say, although there's not usually much to tell them because their child is often quiet and conscientious and, like them, wouldn't say boo to a goose. As long as you smile at them encouragingly, they leave your table thinking that they've passed the test, and everyone's happy.

Parents that you know too much about

There are a number of situations that can fall into this category. I'd worked in one school for over a year before

I realized that I'd been teaching a fellow teacher's offspring, but it's not uncommon. More of a surprise is when a familiar face from the pub plonks himself down in front of you, but this is a good reason to live a suitable distance away from the catchment area.

Nope, the worst case scenario is when the pupil has told you way too much information about the parent, or you have overheard it when they should have been discussing something lesson-related. Could I ever be comfortable having a pleasant discussion with a man whose son recently revealed to everybody that his dad has a large porno stash at the back of his wardrobe? Or chatting with the mother who has dragged along her latest boyfriend, who I know tells the daughter to eff off down the park when she should be sat at home finishing her coursework? Do I really manage to keep a straight face when confronted with the smartly dressed mother who only last weekend had woken up her children by hammering loudly and drunkenly on their front door, crying to be let in, because she was too pissed to get her key in the lock?

Of course, the worrying thing is that if their child is such a blabber-mouth, what are they sitting there thinking about you ... ?

Well-informed parents

These are another bunch of parents that it's not always a pleasure to deal with. They come armed with statistics and an alarming awareness of acronyms and current teaching policies. In some cases, it's usually only afterwards, when you've patiently explained National Curriculum levels and where their child fits into the scheme of things, that you discover that the father is head of a neighbouring primary school and the mother is an educational psychologist. The worst, though, are those who feel it's their duty to challenge and test you, and hold you personally responsible for not spotting that their child has some rare learning disorder (that they have probably just invented) that you should have addressed in your schemes of work.

I'm all for parents taking an active role in their child's education, but well-informed parents would be all the better well informed if they came to sit in their child's lessons for the day and saw for themselves how their teacher was not crushing their child's enthusiasm, but merely requesting that the little git remove his pen from his ear and sit down.

Letters from parents

A familiar phrase to many teachers these days is, 'My mum'll sue you'. We live in a culture of blame-and-compensation, and personally I blame the USA and all those *Ally McBeal* shows. That's a joke by the way. Well, to an extent.

The view towards teachers has shifted. The last generation with wholesale respect for authority figures has grown up, while the children currently punching each other in any school's corridors tend to be the spawn of parents whose main hobbies seem to be watching *Jerry Springer* and expecting something for nothing. They don't support school policies but instead rankle against them, siding with their mega-brats every time. As detentions can now be disputed, the naughtiest kids wriggle out of their punishments by brandishing a note from somebody at home (mum, dad's latest girlfriend, step-gran, etc.).

Having met some of these parents, I imagine they were frequent detention attenders themselves. You know that some parents like to live out their unfulfilled ambitions through their kids? We tend to picture the pushy parents sending their little angels to ballet classes and tennis lessons, but there's also a flip-side to this – the nasty pieces of work who now exact revenge on the teaching profession in remembrance of canings past. It may be very tempting to write a curt reply to a rude note accusing you of picking on their precious offspring, but always keep in mind that your words may be used as evidence against you!

Top tips

Letters from parents require special attention. Especially when they are full of the types of howlers you normally see in the children's work. A letter from home can give you a good insight into the child's home life, from the type of paper used to the contents within. But be careful not to assume too much!

Keep all correspondence you receive. This will probably feature most of all in your role as a form teacher. There will be reasons for absences, notes of upcoming appointments, requests for permission to miss PE or wear trainers instead of proper shoes, explanations and clarifications.

Initial and date each letter. If you have the time, file the letter somewhere safe, unless it's one required by the office as proof of absence.

If the letter requires a reply, remember that many schools prefer that you run your reply past a senior member of staff before sending it home to a parent. For anything more than a quick note, make a photocopy of the letter, whether that's for future reference, or for when the pupil comes to you sheepishly saying that they lost the letter. Keep the letter polite and to the point, whatever style the original is written in. Don't assume that a note scrawled on the back of a flyer is from somebody who doesn't know what writing paper looks like; assume instead it's from a parent governor who was in a terrible rush that morning. If this sounds snobby then it's done its job of making you more aware of any preconceptions you may have.

Remember, you may not feel particularly professional when a child is waving a note in your face as you're halfway down calling the register and trying to prevent the next class from surging in, but if you keep things looking professional this will minimize any possible comeback on yourself.

The school run

Driving to work is usually, thankfully, a non-event. It's a necessity, because there's no way I could struggle home on the bus with three sets of exercise books begging to be marked; a fact I'd love to point out to every environmentalist who glares at my car of just one occupant. Not that I've ever noticed environmentalists glare, just rain-sodden hitchhikers who wouldn't understand my need for half an hour of solitude, loud music and bad singing to blot out the day's events.

Sometimes, though, something does happen on my drive in. Something that stirs the primeval anger known as road rage. It's those mornings that the first child I see bouncing a football in the corridor, running off with someone else's bag, or fiddling with light switches, will be the recipient of a vitriolic verbal blast. Yes, I do feel guilty afterwards. But they did know the risk when they broke the rules.

One morning, though, a road rage incident left me unusually subdued. With only two minutes before the morning meeting, I really didn't need any hold-ups. So picture my frustration when a father in his *de rigeur* 4 × 4 decided to pull across the road in front of me to illegally park on the yellow zigzag lines outside the school. These lines have been painted there to prevent kids like his chauffeured little precious getting knocked over by monster trucks like his. It was this frustration at the moron that made me throw my hands up in incomprehension after I was forced to brake, and then I shouted something rude and most probably highly insulting, as you do when you're in your metal box and nobody else can hear you. Unfortunately, it seemed that moronic father had interpreted my intended message only too well, and now that his monster truck was blocking my escape, he decided he was going to get out and sort me out.

I felt like shouting, 'But I'm a teacher!' as a valid excuse, but in retrospect he would probably have hit me even harder then. However, it must have been my day for lucky endings, as for some reason he climbed back into the moron-mobile, like he realized that being out of his vehicle would involve something called walking, or that it was an experience akin to being wrenched from the womb. It could also have been the oncoming school bus hurtling straight for his moron-mobile now that the bus passengers had been forced off to stream through the school gates, but whatever it was, it saved me from (a) having a slanging match/fisticuffs in the street with a scary idiot in front of the last few stragglers dragging their heels to school, and (b) being late for the staff meeting, which is probably worse.

Top tips

This is one of those unfortunate times when unless the school policy is efficient enough to back you up, there's not a lot that you as an individual can do. Except perhaps badger the senior members of staff into cracking down on parents motoring up to the classroom door each morning to save their child waddling the final few steps. Of course every parent wants to know their child has been safely delivered to school, but they don't seem to realize that zooming around the school grounds or parking illegally outside the school gates in their behemoths is exactly the thing causing the problem.

Avoid the gates and grounds in those crucial minutes before school and after school. Some schools insist that staff members leave at least a quarter of an hour after the final bell. If you accept that your school day is now just fifteen minutes longer, you can avoid the chaos of knotted traffic and swarming children, and therefore avoid contributing to a potentially dangerous situation. It also means that if there are angry parents around, you do not leave yourself in a vulnerable position, perhaps where they could confront you when you're alone.

If a parent wants to talk with you, make sure they go through the proper channels of arranging an interview at a time that suits you both. Do not see them alone. It is always better to have another member of staff with you, such as your head of year or a member of senior management. They can act as a peacemaker, provide another viewpoint on a situation, or just be there to back you up! Make sure you write down what is said at the interview. If it could be a contentious issue, ask the parent to sign the record of what happened at the meeting, meaning that they can't change their mind about what happened afterwards if it suits their purpose better.

Don't forget that you too have a responsibility. Make sure you are completely prepared for any meeting, even if the parent claims they just want a little chat. Have your mark book to hand, register of attendance, exercise books, statements from other teachers, box of confiscated toys – anything that will help you to illustrate how their child behaves and is coping.

Even if you know the parent you are meeting with, as it's to do with a school issue you should remain professional, and remember that they have come to see you as a member of staff, and not as the neighbour they see in the supermarket every week.

Dealing with parents doesn't have to be a battlefield, as long as you remember and practise the rules of engagement.

Conclusion

It was never the aim of this book to provide a comprehensive review of life as a teacher. There are too many facets to the job, and too many variables, depending on the subject and age group taught, the type of school, the ethos and efficiency of the school, the number of management points possessed, and the character and motivation of the teacher. In our educational system, not all things are equal, not by a long way.

You may have recognized characteristics of a school you know or a teacher you avoid in the staffroom. Some parts of the book may have raised a smile or made you angry. You may have thought much of the advice is obvious. In which case, I'm glad, because that means you could well be the type of teacher I admire, one who always tries to make the best of a less than perfect situation. I felt compelled to point out solutions and tips that can be forgotten over years of hard graft and in moments of stress.

The idea for this book came from my website, www.rantingteacher.co.uk, which I set up to save myself banging my head repeatedly against a brick wall. Instead of venting my frustrated spleen to an audience of friends with raised eyebrows and pints in hand, I could let it explode in hyperspace. Judging by the responses I regularly receive, mostly from teachers of course, I'm not alone in feeling the frustration that can be experienced when aspects of the job seem beyond our control.

What I have aimed to do is highlight some of the experiences of a bog-standard classroom teacher, and then suggest ways to regain some control of your own professional life and personal well-being. My hope is that you have found something in here to take away with you and mull over, and that you have been reassured that positive solutions can come out of a good old rant. Now go forth and make your job (even) more enjoyable for yourself!